Y0-BZE-838

West Coast Smoke

drew edwards

West Coast Smoke

W
Warwick Publishing Inc.
Toronto Chicago
www.warwickgp.com

West Coast Smoke
The Inside Story on the B.C. Pot Boom
Drew Edwards

© 2000 Fourth George Mediaworks

All rights reserved. No part of this book may be reproduced, stored in a retrieval system or data base, or transmitted in any form or by any means, electronic, mechanical, photocopying, recording, or otherwise, without the prior written permission of the publisher.

We acknowledge the financial support of the Government of Canada through the Book Publishing Industry Development Program for our publishing activities.

ISBN 1-894020-84-7

Published by Warwick Publishing Inc.
162 John Street
Toronto, Ontario M5V 2E5 Canada
www.warwickgp.com

Distributed in the United States by:
LPC Group
1436 West Randolph Street
Chicago, Illinois
60607

Distributed in Canada by:
General Distribution Services Ltd.
325 Humber College Blvd.
Toronto, ON
M9W 7C3

Cover Design: Kimberley Young
Book Design: Clint Rogerson

Printed and bound in Canada

Contents

Preface -9

1 October 15, 1997, The Holy Smoke Culture Shop, Nelson, B.C.:

The Fix Is In -13

2 A Nelson Primer -25

3 Summer, 1968, Sudbury Ontario: Paul D., The Smart Pothead -35

4 Spring, 1997, Front Street, Nelson: The Roust - - - - - - - -41

5 1982, Davie Street, Vancouver:

Frank Scalia learns that drugs are bad - - - - - - - - - - - - -45

6 October 15, 1997: The Bust - - - - - - - - - - - - - - - - - - -51

7 Middlemiss -59

8 The Dope Swami -75

9 The Defenders: Suffredine and Skogstad do the law thing - - -83

10 Tuesday, November 17, 1997: Murder, Mayhem, Marijuana - -93

11 Trial and Error -103

12 Ernie Miller -109

13 The Decision -117

14 Dope 101 -123

15 Cops and the Finger in the Dam - - - - - - - - - - - - - - -129

16 The Big Bad Americans -141

17 The Industry -149

18 Cases in Point -153

19 The Bad Craziness of Couriers - - - - - - - - - - - - - - - -171

20 The Battlefield of Youth - - - - - - - - - - - - - - - - - - -181

21 Doctor Dope -189

Conclusion and Epilogue -201

Preface

This is not a book promoting the cultivation, trafficking or consumption of marijuana. Nor is it a preachy, Nancy Reagan–style "just say no" rant. It is investigative journalism. Whatever comes across as ludicrous or flagrant on either side of the argument appears that way based upon fact. The world of marijuana cultivation in rural British Columbia is complex and not subject to the usual cops and criminals stereotypes. My aim was to capture this in all its bizarre splendor.

A few disclaimers. Striking a balance while writing this thing was, at times, difficult. As the editor of the local newspaper, I have regular contact with both law enforcement agencies and, to a lesser degree, those directly involved in the marijuana scene. But because I live in the community in which the majority of this story is based, I have been careful in spots not to go overboard with my critical thinking — I still have to live here once this thing comes out. I will say that I have done my best to call it as I see it, regardless of the consequences, but the fact that I know personally, and will continue to know, most of the people featured in this book no doubt affected its outcome.

I will also say that they are, almost universally, interesting, smart, engaging people who are passionate about their beliefs. I gained respect for both cops and dopers while writing this book.

My own personal views on marijuana, however, have not been substantially affected. Having always taken a "live and let live" approach to these issues, I have seen nothing to change my mind. I have smoked dope in my life— I feel it's only fair to confess up front— but, like most journalists, my drug of choice is a long-neck Sleeman's accompanied by a steak sandwich. Marijuana makes me sleepy.

A note about how this book was written: Many of the sources, for obvious reasons, have had their identities changed or protected in the final version. I have used people's true identities wherever possible. In addition, some situations and conversations were re-created for narrative effect. Accuracy and truth, noble pursuits that they are, are slippery to obtain. In some cases accuracy may have been compromised but the overall truth was maintained. In short, I believe this book to be a fair depiction of what goes on in the marijuana world around here.

Finally, some acknowledgments: I am eternally grateful to the Dustin "Sunflower" Cantwell, Paul DeFelice and Alan Middlemiss, the founders of the Holy Smoke Culture Shop, for their time and willingness to speak frankly about their lives. I am also indebted to the members of the Nelson City Police and the Nelson RCMP for their time and trust. I am also thankful to the countless growers, traffickers and users that took the risk in talking to me about what they do and the lives they lead. Their courage made this book possible. Note to law enforcement agents: the day I submitted my final manuscript I burned every audio and note I had and deleted all my rough drafts from my hard drive.

Some others that deserve credit for making this happen: my crew at the *Nelson Daily News,* Bob, Darren, Lara, Bruce and John for their support, my friend Jeremy Mercer for his help in getting this published, the crew at Warwick for their patience and prodding, and to my family, particularly my wife Nicola who helped me through the sometimes painful process of making this dream a reality. Finally to my friend The Fisherman, your guidance and inspiration were key in making this work. Thank you to all.

I hope you enjoy *West Coast Smoke.* In the words of my idol, H.S.T., "*Res Ipsa Loquiter:* let the thing speak for itself."

1

October 15th, 1997,
The Holy Smoke Culture Shop,
Nelson, B.C.: The Fix Is In

Dustin "Sunflower" Cantwell took a huge hit off the bong that was sitting in the middle of the table. He was half standing, leaning out over the edge of the table. He was mobile because the bong wasn't. It was a giant glass globe sitting on a substantial brass base. The top was brass as well, ornate and decorative with a colorful cloth covering to the plastic tube, the other end of which was attached to Dustin's mouth. A friend had picked it up in India and shipped it back to him. Or maybe it was Thailand. Christ, who could be sure?

He sat back down in his chair. Mmmm, yummy. Better than Corn Flakes for this hour in the morning, sometime around 11:30 a.m. The store had just opened. He stared across the table at the first two "customers" for the Holy Smoke

Marijuana Culture Shop that day. They were passing their own joint back and forth to each other, a nice big fatty they'd rolled for themselves. He knew them from around, as two of the several hundred semi-regulars that wandered in and out of the store and in and out of town. Dwayne was one guy's name, with the long red hair, and the other guy's name was Charlie.

Dustin felt he should really get to work, doing something. Clean the store maybe. Update the books. Check the rolling paper supply. What he needed to do was get off his ass and do anything before he ended up macraméed to his goddamn chair by the force of the THC. One more hit and then he'd get to work.

Dwayne took a final a drag on what was left of his joint and stubbed the rest into the ashtray on the table beside the bong. Charlie stuffed the plastic sandwich bag containing the rest of the dope he had brought into his pants pocket.

"See you later, Sunflower," said Charlie.

"Yeah man, be cool," said Dustin through clenched teeth. He waved and let the final remnants of the marijuana smoke out of his lungs. This day was looking good already.

Nelson City Police Det. Ernie Miller peered through the dirty window towards the entrance of the Holy Smoke shop across the alley, just off to his left. He watched 18-year-old Dwayne Williams and 19-year-old Charles Pullen exit the shop. He picked up his walkie-talkie and pressed the transmit button.

"Frank?" he said.

"Yeah" responded Sgt. Frank Scalia.

"Those two guys just left the shop."

"The two from before?"

"Yeah."

Scalia looked down at the screen of his computer inside the unmarked gray Crown Victoria which sat a half a block down the street from the end of the alley that housed Holy Smoke.

Pullen, Charles D., from Calgary, Alberta, with two previous arrests for marijuana possession and one conviction for PPT — possession for the purpose of trafficking — for which he was currently on 12 months' probation — God bless Alberta sentencing. He certainly wouldn't have got that here in B.C. Nothing of what the computer screen told him was surprise. He'd read it months earlier when he'd seen Pullen on the street just days after Charlie came into town.

On that evening, Scalia saw Pullen as a face that he'd never seen before in this city of 10,000. Unwashed, dreadlocked and dressed like a Salvation Army catalog candidate, Pullen looked a lot like the hundred-plus people residing or passing through Nelson, British Columbia at any given time. It was a town with a large transient population, a product of the seasonal work — tree planting in the summer, lifty at the ski hill in the winter — and the fact Nelson had gained almost a Canada-wide reputation as a great place to hang out. But Scalia had good eyes for fresh faces. He was sure he'd never seen the kid who was currently walking by himself up one of Nelson's steep residential streets. At that hour, near 11 p.m., those streets were empty.

15

Scalia had pulled his cruiser over to the curb just in front of the kid and stepped out. Charlie glanced over and quickened his pace as he passed the squad car. Scalia, on this warm August night, was in full Nelson City Police uniform.

"Hey," said Scalia. He used his cop tone, the one that gets people's undivided attention. Charlie stopped and faced Scalia. The cop was 6' 1", five inches taller than Charlie, and he had the cop's short haircut, the cop look and the cop attitude. Having seen this act before, Charlie opted for polite.

"Yes, officer, is there a problem?"

"C'mere a minute," Scalia beckoned. "Got any ID?"

"Why?"

"Because I asked you for ID."

Charlie started to get a little pissed. Cops were always the same, hassling you for no reason except walking down the street. Polite was waning.

"Are you harassing me, officer?" he asked, using the most civil tone possible under the circumstances.

Scalia smiled slightly. A wise-guy — his favorite. "Okay, what's your name then?"

"Charlie." Lying to cops is very bad, Charlie knew.

"Okay Charlie, here's the deal. Either you give me some ID or I decide that I saw you throw a joint away as I drove up. If I saw you throw a joint away, then I have reason to stop and search you. If I search you and find marijuana, or anything else funny on your person, then Charlie, we have ourselves a problem. Or you could just give me some ID and we could have a little chat in my car over here," Scalia said.

Charlie thought this over. He had a couple of joints in a cigarette pack at the bottom of the small canvas bag he had slung over his shoulder. The cop might find them, he might not. Charlie knew, however, that he was on probation and if the cop found the j's and decided to break his balls, he could be looking at some cell time.

"Jesus." Charlie fished his wallet out of his bag and walked toward the car. Scalia opened the passenger side of the front seat and gestured for Charlie to get in. He walked around the driver's side and got in. As Charlie handed him an expired Alberta's driver's license, Scalia turned on the computer and spun the screen towards himself, out of Charlie's view.

"From Alberta, eh?"

"Yes."

"Whatcha doing here in Nelson?"

16

"Visiting friends."

"Staying long?"

"Dunno yet."

"Gotta job?"

"Nope."

Scalia stopped typing and looked at Charlie. Charlie looked back at Scalia. He knew what the cop was thinking.

Useless, no-job, welfare-collecting, dope-smoking, sack of skin. Your government check might as well come right off my goddamn pay stub.

Charlie also had some thoughts of his own.

Tight-ass, rednecked, ball-busting, moron. You wouldn't know the Charter of Rights and Freedoms if the framed version fell and split your pig skull wide open.

The computer beeped.

"Well, well, what's this? Charles Dimitri Pullen, you have a police record. For marijuana," Scalia said with some sarcasm.

"That dope wasn't mine, man," Charlie said with a little smile, joking with the cop a little.

Scalia smirked back. "Of course it wasn't. Either time."

"You got it."

Scalia's face turned serious. "Chuckie, let me explain some-thing to you. This town is a nice town. People are nice, law-abiding citizens with families and jobs and bills to pay. They like a safe, quiet town and we, the members of the Nelson City Police, take pride in giving them just that. With me so far?"

Charlie just looked on and waited.

"What that means is keeping the undesirable elements down and away from the townspeople. We understand that this town has a reputation for dope. We're not stupid. But what I'm saying is that we, the members of the Nelson City Police, do everything we can to prevent people in the town from being concerned. It has a lot to do with profile. Do you know what profile is, Chuck?"

Charlie nodded.

"Know what keeping a low profile is Chuck?"

Charlie nodded.

"That's good. You keep a low profile, stay out of trouble and you get to enjoy your stay here in this beautiful town. You make any noise — one fucking sound—" he paused and his voice took a nasty edge, "—and you'll wish you'd never come here."

The words hung there for a moment and Charlie, despite himself, swallowed once.

"Do we understand each other?"

Charlie nodded.

"Answer me."

"Yes officer."

"Good. Charlie, my name's Frank. It was nice talking to you," Scalia said and gave the kid a great big smile. "Enjoy Nelson."

Charlie got out of the car and continued up the street. Scalia watched him go and hoped his speech had the intended effect. He knew it might stick for a day or two, but that he'd probably see the kid again.

Charlie looked back once at the squad car and saw Scalia wave. Fucking asshole. He took a deep breath and tried to shake it off. Cops were all talk anyway, weren't they? He tried to forget about it. He definitely needed a joint.

Charlie had just received the "Scalia handshake", the Nelson City Police's answer to the Welcome Wagon for losers.

‖ ‖ ‖

Scalia thought of that conversation as he watched Charlie and Dwayne come out the alley and walk down the street on the opposite side, towards him. He'd dealt with Charlie and his new buddy a couple times lately. They were at a house party he broke up two weekends ago, a gathering at a notorious flop house for transients. The cops had walked in after getting permission from the absentee landlord, a local real estate guy who lived on the other side of town from his rundown property.

The place had been so thick with dope smoke they almost called the fire department because they thought something was alight. There was much chaos in the house as those carrying weed made for the back door post-haste. Ernie and Frank had just let them go. Their only mission was to break up the party. To bust all the dope fiends in that place would have required more cars and cells than the NCP had. But there was Charlie, sitting cross-legged on the couch, looking as worried as a deeply stoned man could as Scalia walked in. But Scalia just winked at him, just to remind him he hadn't forgotten.

Dwayne and Charlie crossed the street down from Scalia's undercover spot and headed toward the city's main drag, Baker Street. As they waited at the lights, Scalia radioed Miller.

"Ernie, I'm going to have a chat with those guys; sit tight."

"10-4"

Scalia got out of his car and followed as the two headed along Baker. They turned into the Subway shop half a block down.

Munchies, thought Scalia.

Five minutes later Dwayne and Charlie emerged carrying wax paper–covered, six-inch cold cut combos. As they started down Baker Street, Scalia stepped from the entranceway next to the Subway.

"Hey guys." The two stopped in their tracks. "Let's go in here and have a chat." He opened the door which led into a small foyer, the entrance to the stairs leading to businesses on the second floor of building. Dwayne and Charlie looked at one another, paralyzed by Scalia's sudden presence between bites.

"Now." Scalia's tone got them moving and they stepped into the foyer.

"Up against the wall. Right now."

"What? Why?"

"Do it now!" Scalia's voice rose in volume and pitch. He was trying to get across that he wasn't messing around.

"Jesus Christ," groaned Charlie, putting his sub on the stairs and assuming "the position," hands and feet apart on the wall of the foyer. Dwayne wordlessly followed suit.

"You assholes stink like dope," said Scalia as he began patting Dwayne down, pulling coins, scraps of paper and lots of lint from his ratty jeans.

"Washed these lately?" asked Scalia, not expecting and not receiving an answer. Finding little of interest on Dwayne, Scalia searched Charlie and quickly found the plastic sandwich bag in his pocket.

"Whoops," said Scalia. He stood up, unrolled the baggie and smelled the green, leafy substance.

"Could be oregano, could be weed." He smelled it again, this time taking a deep breath through his nose. He smiled at Charlie.

"Definitely weed."

20

"Fuck." Charlie turned away from the wall and looked at Scalia, who was still grinning like some Cheshire police cat. Dwayne, still too afraid to move, stayed against the wall.

"Well boys, what we have here is a situation. Right now I could bust you—" he pointed at Charlie "—for possession. Which of course would violate your probation. Back to the can for you." He turned to Dwayne, still pinned against the wall. "As for your buddy, I could try and stick him with possession as well."

"Don't listen to him, Dwayne, he can't do fuck-all to you."

Scalia took a single step towards Charlie so the kid's nose was only inches from his chest. Charlie had to strain his neck to see his face. The smile was gone. "I would suggest, considering your predicament, that you shut your face." Scalia stared down hard until Charlie looked away.

"Whatever."

Scalia stepped back. "But instead of making your lives extremely difficult, perhaps we can help each other. I'm going to ask you some questions and if you help me then I'll help you. OK?" Neither of them said a word, so Scalia just began his questions.

"So you guys were at Holy Smoke this morning." He phrased it like a statement.

"No man, not today," said Charlie.

"Listen peckerhead, I just fucking watched you come out of there and down to the Subway."

"Oh."

"'Oh' is right. Let's try it again: so you guys were at Holy Smoke this morning."

"Yeah," Charlie said as Dwayne nodded in agreement.

"Smoke a little weed?"

Dwayne cleared his throat, finally taking his hands off the wall and slowly turning to face Scalia.

"A little," he said.

"You guys buy it there?"

"Un uh, nope," said Charlie.

"No lying."

"I'm serious, man. I brought it with me. You can't buy there."

"Never?"

"Well, maybe some guys do, but I've never seen it, or even heard of it." Charlie was trying to give the asshole cop what he wanted, without fucking his friends over. It was a shaky rope to walk.

"Hmmm." Scalia pondered this. "Was there other dope there that you saw?"

Charlie shrugged.

"Was there?"

Dwayne was watching Charlie intently, trying to follow his lead. Charlie just shrugged again.

Scalia stepped forward and grabbed Charlie by the jacket. "Okay fucko, it's back to the can with you, let's go." Scalia reached for his cuffs. Dwayne looked panicked. "I hope they've cleaned the puke out of the cell from last night, some guy had dirty Chinese before he drank himself stupid. It sure stank."

"OK, OK, OK. Jesus Christ. Yes there was dope there. One of the owners was smoking up with us with his own weed." Charlie gently shook loose for Scalia's grip.

"Which one?"

"Sunflower."

"Cantwell?"

Charlie nodded.

"Were the others there?"

"No man, just him, far as I saw."

Scalia thought about this. "You guys smoke up in there often?"

Dwayne found his tongue, feeling guilty about letting Charlie take all the heat. "No sir, they don't really like people smoking up there all the time. Bad for business and too risky."

"Why today then?"

"Well sir, it's still pretty early, you know? Probably figured it was OK." Dwayne paused, looking over at Charlie. "I guess it wasn't."

"Show me some ID" Scalia took Dwayne's wallet and wrote down as much information on him as he could gather from the rumpled, sweaty documents within.

"OK, this is what's gonna happen," he said pointing at Dwayne. "You are going to make yourself disappear for the rest of the day. No talking to your buddies and no going anywhere near that store. You may or may not receive a summons on the possession charge. If you keep quiet today and keep your nose clean from now on, the odds improve greatly that you won't get any nasty mail. Do we understand each other?"

"Yes sir."

"I mean it, you go near that store I'll be all over you like a dirty shirt. And we're watching, got me?" Scalia stared hard at him.

"Yes sir."

"Now get the fuck out of here." Dwayne hit the door running, not looking back and leaving his sandwich on the stairs. Scalia turned to Charlie and reached for his cuffs.

"And you're coming with me."

"What! You said —" Charlie took a step back, banging into the wall.

"Yeah, yeah." Scalia spun him around and put his hands behind his back.

"But, but—"

"Listen, you may get out of this still, I just need some more help."

"But you said..." Charlie's voice dropped off, knowing he was beaten. Scalia began to read him his Charter rights as he opened the door and guided Charlie onto Baker.

23

"You have the right to retain and instruct counsel without delay..." By the time they returned to Scalia's unmarked sedan, he was all done. He unlocked and guided Charlie's head under the door frame of the rear seat. He picked up his radio.

"Ernie, still there?"

"Yep."

"Everything OK?"

"Well I just saw a bunch of young kids go in there, 15-and 16-year-olds." Miller's voice had an edge of concern. His daughter was around that age.

"They're smoking pot in there, Ernie."

"Those guys told you?"

"Yeah."

"Bastards. Frank, we have to do something. There's kids in there."

"I gotta drop a package at the station. Meet me on the street in 10 minutes."

"OK."

Scalia started the engine and began the two-block drive to the one and only Nelson City Police Station. He was pissed. Kids for god's sake. These guys were going down today, no fucking doubt about it now.

2

A Nelson Primer

Nelson, British Columbia, is the marijuana culture capital of North America. Per Capita, more people grow dope, smoke dope and are influenced by dope life here than in any other place known to man. Marijuana is woven into the way of life, a social stimulator, an economic generator. Ask the cops, they'll say it's true. Ask the politicians, ask the potheads, ask the kids, ask the 45-year-old professionals, they'll all say the same thing: Nelson, this charming little mountain town, is Dope Central.

But like any good dope hideout, it's tough to get to. It is situated in the southern interior of British Columbia — the dope province of Canada — about equal driving distance from Vancouver and Calgary. More importantly, the U.S. border is only an hour to the south.

Driving to Nelson from the West, there are two major mountain passes to traverse or one mountain pass and one ferry ride. From the East there are two other passes to manage. There are commercial flights to a city a half hour away, but they are not for the faint of heart. Small airplanes, roller coaster turbulence and no bathrooms can be a struggle for the uninitiated traveler used to plush seats, movie screens and a full service bar.

The door to the cockpit on these flights is often wide open, and on a good day with crystal-clear, bright sunshine, the Selkirk Mountains that surround Nelson for miles and miles on each side look as if they've been chiseled just yesterday, they are so fresh and vibrant. These mountains get a little close when the plane swings in to land. The nose angles toward them, closer and closer, until the plane is literally lower than the mountain tops. It seems like the plane is crashing, slowly and deliberately, into the vast expanse of rock and trees spread around it. At what seems the last second, the pilot veers hard to the right and plops the bird on the tarmac, which appears from out of nowhere.

Stepping out of the plane, the mountains are all around, their tops covered in snow. They are stunning. It smells good. The air seems to have more oxygen content than regular city air. It is infinitely breathable.

The Castlegar terminal is two counters, a coffee shop and … well that's pretty much it. Travelers to Nelson often take something called the Queen City Limousine which runs twice a day between Nelson and Castlegar, roughly a half-hour drive. It costs $15 and the running tour commentary is included if the passenger isn't from around here. The Queen City Limousine is a gray Econoline van.

With a little luck the driver will explain the concept of "Kootenay Time." The Kootenays is the name for the general area around Nelson, roughly four or five hours in all directions. It is a derivative of the Kutenai Indians who settled farther south in Washington State along the Columbia River. There are East and West Kootenays as well.

"Kootenay Time is the pace of life here — nice and slow. Things happen when they happen and nobody gets too worked up about it," the driver will say.

Give an example.

"OK, so you have a leaky pipe, right? You call the plumber and you say, 'When can you be here?' And he says, 'Well, I can probably make it Wednesday.' But it's only Monday today and you know the damn fool doesn't have enough business to keep him busy until Wednesday. But that's the way it is, that's just when he wants to do it. He's operating on Kootenay Time."

Don't people get pissed off?

"Well, city folks usually do at first. They get frustrated. They walk past people on the street because they're going so fast and the locals are going at their own, easy pace. But they adjust to it, learn to love it too."

The drive to Nelson follows the headwaters of the Kootenay River along a twisting two-lane highway, past hydro-electric projects, a lumber mill, a couple of volunteer fire stations and lots of well-spaced houses. Finally it reaches an opening at the base of three mountains with a small lake at the bottom. The city rises up on the gentle slope of two of the mountains; the third, Elephant Mountain, looms over the far side of the lake and the city. From the highway, a great deal of the city is visible. Set against the mountains and the lake, it looks pretty.

27

The highway loops down to the base of the main drag, Baker Street. It is four blocks of mostly retail space with lots of stone buildings and cloth awnings. Though there is a mall with a big box store three blocks to the south, Baker Street is still the main hub of town. It is a stark contrast from the big city: no neon and no burger joints.

The majority of Nelson's commercial and retail space is found on the streets parallel to Baker, Vernon and then Front Street. Included on those strips are the Heritage Inn, a 100-year-old refurbished hotel two former prime ministers have stayed in – and home to three of the city's three-dozen or so bars and restaurants – and the Civic Centre, the 80-year-old recreation facility that also houses the city's only movie theatre.

Nelson was settled 100 years before as a logging and mining center, like most towns in the region. The town grew quickly, and pretty soon there were 10,000 people in Nelson, almost the same number as there are today. It developed into a hub for government and transportation as the Canadian Pacific Railroad set up shop on the waterfront, a few kilometers down from the saw mill. The place boomed for decades.

Over the years, Nelson developed a rather unique social make-up. Many of the families who live here have done so for generations, and they feel a sort of ownership. It's almost as if there is some kind of residency requirement to be taken seriously.

Along with the usual Anglo-Scottish-Irish contingent, Nelson has significant Chinese and Italian populations. Distinctive elements in the area's cultural mix are the descendants of Russian immigrants known as Doukhobours. Essentially, they are God-fearing people who got kicked out of Russia after the revolution because they were God-fearing people. Ironically, they are so God-fearing that they keep a minimum of personal possessions, living an almost communal, Amish-like lifestyle. One of the Doukhobour sects, the Sons of Freedom, were radical political activists.They blew up bridges, appeared in court naked, burned their own houses to demonstrate their anti-materialism. Many Doukhobours live "Up the Valley," which refers to the Slocan Valley, halfway between Castlegar and Nelson.

In the 1960s, the Doukhobours got some new neighbors: draft-dodging American refugees. Only an hour from the Idaho and Washington State borders, the Valley quickly became known as a beautiful place where communal living was possible. There was a minimum of cops, just a bunch of crazy Russians who were as politically radical and back to the earth as they were. Perfect. This is where Nelson's dope culture originated, and to this day, "the Valley" is notorious for it's grow operations (known locally as "grow ops").

The city of Nelson, in the meantime, was still doing well as a mill town and as a center of government, where most of the regional offices for the province and the feds were set up. There was even a small post-secondary school, Notre Dame University, and life was pretty good.

And then the punch in the crotch known as the 1980s arrived. The mill closed and there was no industry to replace it. The university was shut down by the province. The population of Nelson plunged from 10,000 to around 7,500 for the first time in 85 years, and property values dropped like a stone. Nelson was dying.

29

In the early-to-mid-1980s, as things approached their worst, a few of the local leaders realized a radical change was necessary if they were going to save their town. No longer able to depend on the land to support them, they came up with a plan. Looking at old photos, they realized Nelson's main drag, Baker Street, consisted mostly of stone and brick buildings which had, with the onslaught of the bad architecture of the 60s and 70s, been covered up with all kinds of stucco, aluminum siding and crappy neon signs. With a huge heap of cash from the governments (plural), they went about restoring Baker Street to all its old glory. Presto — one very beautiful, heritage-themed downtown. The tourists started to trickle in and the town exodus stabilized.

The newly-dubbed "Heritage City" got a huge boost in 1986 when *Roxanne* came to town. The Steve Martin, Daryl Hannah Americanization of *Cyrano de begerac* was filmed over a two-month period and featured tons of pretty shots of the town Nelson had become. The fire hall, the beautiful house Hannah lives in, the gorgeous downtown – all featured prominently. The climactic final fire scene was filmed in the parking lot next to the *Daily News*. The film, which did reasonably well at the box office and even better on video, had two effects: it was a huge boost for the flagging confidence of the town, and it doubled tourism virtually overnight. A 30-foot mural of Martin still graces Front Street, just off the downtown.

Slowly Nelson was developing a reputation as a great place to live. A community post-secondary school, Selkirk College, and an art school, Kootenay School of the Arts, were established. An old playhouse, the Capitol, was restored as a community project, and Nelson began its next life as an artsy enclave. CBC Radio host Vicki Gabereau did remote broadcasts from the Capitol and author John Villani christened it the best small arts town in Canada in his book *The 100 Best Small Arts Towns in America* (it was ranked number five overall). Additionally, the local ski hill, Whitewater, started to develop an international reputation for big-ass powder and that drew the young kids and the Aussies to spend the winters.

In short, Nelson became a lifestyle town. It was set among the mountains, with a heritage-themed downtown, a blooming art scene and a slew of things to do, like golf and ski. It started to draw yet another kind of folk to follow the Nelson-lifers and the hippies: the big city refugees. Essentially these were people, often couples, who simply got sick of the rat race and decided to try the "Kootenay-Time" pace of Nelson. They came primarily from California, Calgary and Vancouver, but also from Ontario and the East.

The typical story goes something like this: Jon and his family are driving to the West Coast from their home in Calgary on a vacation and stop in Nelson. They love it here, and upon returning home, Jon, an investment banker, and his wife Cathy, a teacher, realize how meaningless and empty their lives are. So they quit their jobs and come to Nelson. Cathy gets a teaching job for far less money and Jon works as a snowboard instructor in the winter and a greens keeper at an area golf course in the summer. They go to the Capitol Theatre once a month for local plays or a jazz band. Their kids attend Waldorf School, an alternative teaching program focusing on holistic learning. They have no money — relative to their life in Calgary — but they are infinitely happier. This is a story told over and over and over again: Nelson is place where you come when your soul is broken and you don't know why.

Slowly but surely as these urban refugees arrived, Nelson became this cool, chic little place. The hippies in the Valley got older, got jobs, but still clung to their principles by joining organic vegetable co-ops and naming their kids Rainbow, Waterfall and Sky. And the Nelson-lifers made a killing in real estate. The families who had been here for generations didn't leave when the going got tough – they just bought a bunch of cheap property. When Nelson regained its strength and became a cool place, with all these urban refugees moving to town, the lifers made a mint. Real estate values soared from the early 1980s to the millennium. With little or no room for expansion (remember the town is built into the side of three mountains), the housing market in Nelson was and is a sellers' market.

31

But this rather eclectic mix of people has created quite the political dichotomy. The Nelson-lifers and the remaining ethnic families who own most of the established businesses (car dealerships, real estate agencies, restaurants) as well as most of the remaining developable property are notoriously conservative in nature. The urban refugees and hippy folks are far more liberal, needless to say. It makes for interesting politics. On a federal level, the MP is a slick, Cadillac-driving, right-wing Alliance member named Jim Gouk. Provincially, the MLA is an American expatriate (and falsely rumored draft dodger) from the Valley named Corky Evans who drops his g's when he talks about farmin' and fishin'. Corky is NDP (Canada's far left party) and the furthest possible thing from the slick political animal that is Jim Gouk.

This strange political split also plays itself out locally. In November of 1996, Nelson went through one of the most acrimonious, piss and vinegar, nasty-ass municipal elections ever held. On one side was the incumbent mayor, Gary Exner, a local accountant who had won a by-election after the sitting mayor resigned when it was reported in the Vanouver papers that he had been dialing 1-900 sex numbers from city hall. Exner was the conservative, pro-business, right wing candidate who was tight with the Nelson-lifers. He talked about "getting things done" and "preserving our families." On the left was a card-carrying NDP member Donna Macdonald, an urban refugee. She was a freelance writer who worked in MLA, Corky Evan's constituency office. She talked about "community decision-making" and "vision for our future."

The two candidates disliked each other intensely. There was talk of sleazy politics on both sides, from Donna stuffing ballot boxes (never proven) and business owners threatening their employees if they didn't vote for Gary (also never proven). It came to a head when someone quietly hung Gary in effigy in the middle of the night from the roof of his own garage and put a potato in the tailpipe of his Jeep Cherokee. It was never connected to Donna, but the general feeling was things had gone too far.

Gary won the election by 700 votes in a turnout of over 77 per cent — unheard of for a municipal election. The council, however, was divided between conservatives and liberals, and it set the stage for the most bizarre three years the town had ever seen.

There is one more interesting element of Nelson: it has its own municipal police force. The Nelson City Police is the smallest city police force in British Columbia. Most B.C. towns of this size are policed by the Royal Canadian Mounted Police, and in fact Nelson has a regional detachment office of RCMP cops as well. They look after the highways, the outlying areas outside the city limits and the small towns within a few hours of Nelson. The RCMP rotate every few years — Nelson City Police are permanent fixtures.

What does this mean? Well, it means most of the cops in the NCP have been here a long time. Many have worked in larger centers and then applied to get out of the dirty city. It also means they know every small-time and big-time crook in the area. For example, a local shop was broken into several times over the period of a few months and had various small items stolen, the most significant being a portable radio. Each and every time the NCP not only caught the suspects, but returned the radio to its rightful owner. Great police work? Sort of. It was the same bunch of kids every time. In a city of 10,000 there are only so many petty criminals, so many juvenile delinquents. The cops know them all. The point is, there is a personal relationship between the NCP and the city of Nelson. They aren't just cops, they are neighbors, friends, and in the case of the crooks, nemeses. It's an interesting relationship.

33

"Interesting relationship": as good a term as any to sum up Nelson as a whole. It is a place with a colorful past and an even more colorful present. It is an ecclectic convergence of lifestyles, people and politics, mixed together with the power of the mountains and a strange energy that is beyond explanation.

3

Summer, 1968, Sudbury, Ontario: Paul D., The Smart Pothead

One fine afternoon, 11-year-old Paul DeFelice was hanging around the Catholic school playground next to his house, the place where all the older neighborhood kids came to congregate. One of them had a piece of hash he'd gotten from his biker older brother. So they've got it, but nobody knows how to smoke it. This is Sudbury, Ontario, in 1968, the height of the hippie, dope-smoking times — but Sudbury in the 60s was more like Milwaukee in the 1950s, with its conservative, working class ethic. Paul, small for his age, with glasses and a geeky demeanor, had seen an illustration showing how you put a piece of hash on a pin and smoke it with a Bic pen. So he tells the older kids and together they figure it out. Finally one of the older kids says "let him have a puff." Right off, Paul likes it. He laughs. He gets silly. Then he gets all paranoid because he looks next door at his house and he remembers he has to go home eventually. But there's no question, he likes it, he likes it a lot.

Paul lived in a predominantly Italian neighborhood, so growing up all the guys liked to look tough. Everybody wore Brylcreem to grease their hair back and kids carried rumble chains and sticks for getting in fights. Paul tried it, but wearing glasses and being a little smaller than the rest of the crowd, he just didn't have it in him, he just wasn't one of the tough guys. He tried though, smoking cigarettes, keeping a pack of Export A rolled under his short sleeve t-shirt. He just didn't fit in.

But when Paul was 12 or 13 he became aware of another neighborhood down the road, where kids acted a little differently. They didn't tend to fight; instead they listened to music, liked to recite poetry, dress far-out and act goofy. They also smoked marijuana. He took a liking to it right away. Up until then all his friends drank lots of beer and Paul could never keep up, but now he'd finally found something that he liked; where it used to be that kids would drink him under the table, now he could smoke people under the table. Instead of drinking and fighting and drinking some more, Paul had found kids whose the main source of entertainment was experimenting with drugs, pretending they were high even when they weren't. From his perspective it was just a hell of a lot more fun.

Paul was 16 before he started using marajuana regularly. The main thing was, he couldn't find it — being a young kid, it wasn't readily available for him or anyone in his circle of friends. But by the time he was in his mid-teens, he could go to the pool hall and the bikers would sell to him, or his older sister's boyfriends would try and get in good with little brother by getting him some goods once in a while. But right up until his senior year of high school, Paul was too uncomfortable to smoke it all the time, saving it for weekends. By grade 13 though, he was just going through the motions at school. He didn't want to be there; he was going just to socialize, buying time until he could figure out what he was going to do with his life. He had only three classes, so he started puffing between classes and he started to realize it wasn't so bad. He found he could puff and read and get his homework done, and he even found the subjects more interesting.

By the time he got to Confederation College in Thunder Bay in 1975 Paul was using marijuana regularly. He had these boring, esoteric classes that he had trouble getting into. But he found if he took a couple of puffs, all of a sudden he could learn. He had a personal bud epiphany the night before his first year calculus exam. He'd basically given up, having failed everything up until that point. He stepped out into the parking lot with a friend and smoked some really potent ganja. He came back in and one of the guys starting showing him some answers and, in his state of mind, it started making sense. He did a bunch of sample problems and had it down — he'd just learned calculus. He aced the exam the next day — while high. He took a three-year course in architectural engineering technology — drafting. There were 100 students in first year and only 12 graduated — including Paul D, now a full-blown pothead.

37

Paul doesn't think he's ever been addicted to pot. He's used it a lot and used it continuously but doesn't think he's been addicted. He's been addicted to coffee and quit it. He's been addicted to tobacco smoking for over 25 years before quitting. He's gone for extended periods without pot. He went on a month-long ski trip in Europe with not a single toke the whole time in 88. He went a month without it in 1998 because he was trying to solve a sinus problem, but quitting only made his sinus situation worse. His parents came a few summers ago and he traveled around with them; he could have puffed, but figured being with his parents was trip enough. He tries to save it now for special occasions or as his end of the day relaxer.

Following graduation in 1979, Paul moved to Calgary, Alberta, and worked for a general contractor on huge warehouses and office buildings, and then moved to an architect's office, for better pay and more status. He was clean shaven, wore nice pants and shirts to work and smoked pot pretty much every day. In the early 80s, when the oil industry crashed in Calgary, Paul — along with 300 others — were laid off as 90 per cent of his work was in oil offices and related industries. He took that opportunity to come to Nelson.

Paul's plan was to collect pogey until it ran out and then get back to the real world, either in Calgary or Vancouver. But after a year, he'd learned to like life in Nelson. He was skiing all the time — his other great love after pot. There were some local guys up at Whitewater who were learning how to film and he did some stunts for them. When one of those guys started working for sport-adventure film maker Warren Miller as a cameraman, Paul ended up in three feature-length films and a bunch of home videos.

38

It was also right around the time all the Baker Street renovations were being done. Paul got to know the designers responsible and ended up doing some drawings for them. He developed a reputation for quality drafting. He was not involved with marijuana activism at this point. He smoked pot and experimented with psychedelics and tended to like them, but he was definitely more on the conservative side.

Slowly, Paul became aware of the marijuana subculture in Nelson, getting the feeling that there weren't many people in town that didn't puff. He wondered how the town was surviving. The mill was closed, the university was closed, there was no work and yet there were people buying houses, buying cars, wink wink nudge nudge. Hell, Paul D. figured, if everybody else is growing and getting paid, I might as well too. He started growing a little pot.

In 1985, however, he got busted when his best friend's mother called the police on him. He received a cultivation conviction and he didn't like the way it went down. He'd had only a small operation and wasn't hurting anybody – it seemed stupid that he now had a criminal record. It was right at the beginning of the U.S. government's war on drugs, and pretty soon Paul couldn't get into the States anymore — no more Warren Miller films.

The conviction started him down the road to activism. He started writing letters and getting vocal about the drug laws. In 1988, the Canadian government banned *High Times* magazine for the second time, and Paul couldn't believe that free speech was being so badly trampled. That really got him going. He did a ton of reading and decided he had to come out of the closet – he had to start speaking up for this plant.

For the next eight years, Paul D. became a part-time draftsman and full-time spokesperson for pot. He was also an avid activist for the environment, and was one of the founding partners in the Ecocenter, a local environmental resource center. That success spawned another idea.

39

He and some friends had kicked around the idea that Nelson needed a store to get pipes, rolling papers and that sort of thing. For example, Paul's favorite papers are Club papers: they're pure, light with no glue on them. But he could only get them in Vancouver. They used to kid, "boy we're going to have to start a store just so we can get good papers," never actually thinking they'd be the ones that would start it.

Paul had met Alan Middlemiss in 1990 at a Grateful Dead show in Hamilton, Ontario. He was handing out hemp literature to everyone he met and when he gave a leaflet to Alan, they struck up a conversation. They kept in touch; Alan moved to

Vancouver soon after and made his way to Nelson by 1992. Paul had met Dustin "Sunflower" Cantwell at a Hemp Fest in '92 just outside of Nelson. The three of them would get together and bullshit about hemp activists and joke about starting a store.

When Gary Exner was re-elected as mayor of Nelson in 1996, Paul D. decided they really had to do something. In the term Exner had already done, he had banned dogs, Frisbees, skateboarders, bongos and buskers from the downtown. The municipal government was clamping down on the "alternative lifestylers." Paul and his friends didn't like the way things were going and they needed a way to rally people of like mind, people of their own culture. They had to let Exner know they weren't going away. Plus Cantwell and Middlemiss were getting tired of roofing. Th e hemp store seemed like a good idea for a business, and it would be political action at the same time. The real break came one day when Alan and Dustin walked past a storefront location on Front Street, saw a "For Rent" sign and checked it out. They told Paul to go have a look. He put $100 down right there and called Dustin.

"Guess what? I just did it."

Holy Smoke was born.

4
Spring, 1997, Front St., Nelson: The Roust

Paul DeFelice, Alan Middlemiss and Dustin "Sunflower" Cantwell opened the Holy Smoke Culture Shop in a little 180-square foot shop on Front Street with a small amount of paper and pipes. In an ironic twist, that location was right across the hall from where Narcotics Anonymous held their meetings.

Some of their first visitors were Det. Ernie Miller and Sgt. Kirk Evans of the NCP. They wandered around the tiny store, peering at the shelves, the pot posters and the lone glass case. The police saw the store as an affront, something that didn't belong in their quiet, law-abiding town.

"Good afternoon, officers," said Middlemiss with a big smile. He wasn't overly concerned by the cops' presence — it was to be expected.

"You guys selling dope in here?" Evans asked gruffly.

"No sir," said Middlemiss politely. "Just what you see."

"Sure smells like it."

"That's incense, officer."

"Right. Incense." Evans leaned his burly frame across the counter and stuck his reddened face as close to Middlemiss as he could get it. Alan didn't move.

"'Let me tell you something. You and your shitty store are going down, sooner rather than later. I'm going to see to it."

"But officer, we aren't doing anything illegal. We are selling pipes and papers and literature. What's wrong with that?" Middlemiss asked innocently.

"And what are they supposed to smoke with those pipes and those papers?" Evans was sarcastic.

"Well..." Middlemiss smiled just a little. "Tobacco."

"Don't give me that. You guys are promoting marijuana smoking and we don't like it. Just be warned: you're finished, and soon."

42

With that, Evans and Miller tossed their business cards on the counter. They would soon be prominently displayed in the shop.

The officers of the Nelson City Police kept their collective eyes on the Holy Smoke Culture Shop. There were rumours of drug use in the store and some reports of drug sales, but nothing concrete enough to mount a serious investigation. The store generated a lot of traffic, especially in the first couple of months, as people came to check it out. The store, however, was well off the beaten track of Baker Street and got little drop-in traffic. So when a basement shop came available in Herridge Lane, an alley just a half-block from Baker, the Holy Smokers decided to make the jump — even though it meant making a substantially larger monthly rent payment. They moved to the 700 sq. foot location below the weekly newspaper just two months after opening the Front Street store.

Meanwhile, the head of the Special Investigation Group of the NCP, Sgt. Frank Scalia, put together a memo for his boss, Chief Constable Andrew Oak. It got right to the point in the opening paragraph:

> Since this business was granted a license to operate within the City of Nelson it has been a concern to police as it exists only to promote the illicit consumption of marijuana and its derivatives (cannabis resin or hashish, cannabis oil). These types of outlets have for some time been referred to as "head shops". It has nothing to do with culture and everything to do with the subculture surrounding marijuana and its hallucinogenic effects.

It went on to describe visits by police, how each time officers suspected the owners of the shop had been smoking pot just before the cops arrived. Scalia stated that, in his opinion, a possession bust was possible.

43

> The current reality of the situation, however, is that the labor and costs of investigating and prosecuting minor drug offenses is not justified by the penalties imposed. This does not make it right.
>
> The Holy Smoke Culture Shop, like all other head shops, is operating in a gray area which condones the unlawful consumption of marijuana and borders on criminal sanction. It is not a viable business in the sense that the social impact of its message, increased drug use, can only be negative. There is no doubt that many of the items sold will end up seized by police, from offenders of all ages dealt with in routine complaints and street checks. Hypothetically, cases may arise where the store

owners are subject to criminal charges and seizure for their activities... There is significant concern to this point, however, that a revocation of the [business] license of this store may provide justified civil proceedings.

Scalia had basically taken his red, white and blue paint and slapped a great big bulls-eye on the Holy Smoke Culture Shop and the three guys that ran it.

44

5

1982, Davie Street, Vancouver: Frank Scalia learns that drugs are bad

45

Vancouver Police Department Constable Frank Scalia was working the Davie Street beat in Vancouver in 1982 when a group of 12 or 15 kids in their late teens and early twenties arrived from Quebec. They were loosely associated and they had come to B.C. for the summer to pick fruit in the Okanagan Valley. They eventually ended up in the Davie Street area of Vancouver, one of the tougher parts of town. Some of the guys had marginal criminal records but nothing substantial, and most had brought their girlfriends with them. Scalia and the other officers in his squad dubbed them "the French Connection."

The Quebecois crew started scoping out what they could do in the big city. They easily qualified for welfare and started collecting pogey checks. It wasn't much and it didn't go far, but they soon figured out a way to make their government dollars go further. They got involved in the neighborhood marijuana market — strictly dope and hash. Instead of using their welfare money to pay rent or buy food, they bought marijuana in large quantities, then split it up and sold it in smaller packages on they street. They made a ton of money and it sure beat picking fruit — this money grew on trees. In the meantime they were using their product a great deal, a side benefit enjoyed by most dope dealers.

Scalia and his team busted several members of the French Connection, resulting in brief jail terms. But it didn't work. As soon as they were out again they started right back up — the trade was too lucrative and too attractive. Slowly the Quebeckers moved from Davie Street to the far more rough and tumble Granville Street — ground zero for criminal activity in downtown Van.

Scalia watched as the members of the French Connection slid from dope to harder drugs. They started with the use and trafficking of marijuana to using and selling coke and heroin. Scalia says he remembers talking to one of these fellas, who said that a speedball, the mix of coke and heroin, was absolutely the best thing ever. Within about a year-and-a-half several of the girlfriends were prostitutes, hooking to support their habit and their boyfriends' habit — slaves to narcotics so powerful they'd do anything, absolutely anything, to get it. Out of the 12 or 15 guys and girls that originally made up the French Connection, half of them were dead within three years of drug overdoses. It started innocently enough with marijuana.

46

Scalia had already seen a lot of marijuana before he got to the dirty streets of Vancouver. Growing up in Trail, B.C., about an hour south of Nelson, Scalia had been exposed to the hard-working, hard-partying life that defined the mining-based town. Trail's main employer was Cominco which ran the lead, silver and zinc smelter that fueled the community's economy but also devastated the landscape. Until 1960, the hillsides surrounding the predominantly Italian community were devoid of vegetation, and to this day warnings are issued about lead contamination in the soil.

Many of Scalia's grade school and high school buddies turned to marijuana. A couple of them got into it too much and Scalia watched them lose their motivation, drop out of school and become completely obsessed with dope. It got to the point where nothing else mattered; their whole lives revolved around finding better ways of getting high and disovering better ways of getting really, *super* high. It left an indelible stamp on Scalia. It laid the foundation for his tough, inflexible stance on drugs.

Scalia left Trail for the University of British Columbia and after a year moved on to Simon Fraser University to pursue his degree in criminology. Unlike many others who are exposed to marijuana during their university years, Scalia says he saw less of it there than when he was in Trail. The criminology department was filled with square people pursuing careers as lawyers and, as in Scalia's case, as cops. He graduated with his degree and entered the police academy. He was 22.

47

Scalia says he was fairly liberal when he first went into police work — compared to other cops — but what he saw on the streets of Vancouver changed his opinion. He quickly learned that everything came back to drugs. All the prostitution related back to drugs — generally heroin and cocaine — because the majority of the hookers were addicted. A great number of the major crimes related back to drugs; many of the armed robberies and break and enters were committed by drug addicted people as well. It didn't take Scalia too long to figure out that targeting drugs and drug-addicted individuals was the best way to get at the heart of those other crimes.

Scalia has hundreds of stories like that of the French Connection, stories that start innocently enough with marijuana use and lead to other drugs and other crimes and then, eventually, to tragedy. This is why when people tell him that marijuana doesn't lead them to other things, he doesn't buy it. To Scalia's way of thinking society already has at least two substances that are extremely harmful but legal: alcohol and tobacco. We've all seen the social and medical ills those generate. Why would we want to legitimize a third one, marijuana, he asks. We know it must be bad because the user is ingesting smoke into the lungs which is not the design of the body. Scalia has stats on teen pregnancy rates and can talk at length on the studies done on amotivational syndrome created by ganja. It might be a gateway drug and it might make users susceptible to addiction to other drugs. He is vehemently, viscerally opposed to it.

Scalia brought this hardened, zero-tolerance philosophy into the heart of bud country in 1990. Though he was no longer exposed to the blatant destruction of humanity that is Vancouver's Granville and Davie Streets, Scalia saw Nelson as the precursor to that life — and therefore an even more important battlefield in the war on drugs. He now sees what marijuana does to teens on an almost daily basis. They drop out. They hang out on the corner. He sees 15- and 16-year-old kids in cells at the Nelson City Police station, arrested for B&Es. They're robbing to get money for marijuana.

So Scalia goes to schools and spreads his gospel. It's a simple message: you don't know when you choose to smoke dope if you have an addictive personality or not. Some people have good families and are smart kids but have that addictive personality and it just destroys them. You just don't know. There is a huge risk factor. There's less of a jump from cigarettes to marijuana. There is less of a jump from marijuana to cocaine and other drugs. One minute you're happy with pot and the next you're moving on to other things. He thinks an aggressive campaign in the schools is the key to winning the war on drugs.

The movement towards liberalization angers Scalia. He fully admits he's developed tunnel vision about it. He doesn't want it to get to the point where people feel they can smoke dope openly on the street, something that happens occasionally in Nelson, sometimes in the middle of the day. And don't get him started on medicinal marijuana, the great smokescreen for dope-heads. To his mind pro-marijuana advocates are merely using the medicinal marijuana argument to legitimize thier legalization demands so that they can walk around stoned and high and smoking 24 hours a day.

Scalia would favor an American-style war on drugs. He thinks the minimum sentences and harsh penalties south of the border are great. He's hoping the Yanks will put additional pressure on the Canadian and B.C. governments to toughen things up — or at least get the judiciary to enforce the law by handing down proper sentences. The fact that B.C. has the most lax sentencing record in the country drives him nuts. And Nelson is the worst of all — though he's reluctant to say it publicly.

49

All of this is why Holy Smoke is "Satan's Lair" in Frank Scalia's world. To him it is contributing to the destruction of the social fabric of the community. It's turning kids on to a harmful substance that makes a lifestyle of non-productivity is entirely possible — if not probable. There can be no winners in that equation. By having marijuana popularized, indoctrinating our youth into the marijuana subculture we're all going to be losers. Frank Scalia knows. He's 41 now and in his 18 years wearing a badge he's seen it happen, over and over and over again.

6

October 15, 1997:
The Bust

Six months and thirteen days after Scalia's memo to Chief Oak, Det. Ernie Miller was peering through one-way glass across Herridge Lane at the entrance of Holy Smoke Culture Shop, waiting for his partner Scalia to get back to him. Miller, like Scalia, was sick to death of these guys flouting the law and poisoning kids with their talk — and God knows what else. The group of teens he'd seen enter the store still hadn't come out. His radio beeped.

"Go ahead."

"Ernie, meet me around the corner."

"OK."

Miller slipped away from his surveillance post and moved through the apartment building. He got to the street and quickly looked both ways. It was hard being a plain-clothes cop in a small town where pretty much everybody knew you by your first name. But nobody noticed Miller on this day, just another pair of blue jeans and a leather jacket heading to work or down the street for a coffee. He found Scalia in the unmarked car around the corner.

"Frank, those kids are still inside."

"OK. Shit."

"I've had enough of these guys. It's time to put a stop to it. What did those punks say?" asked Miller.

"That they were smoking up in the store, but with their own weed. I found some on one of them. He's at the station writing up his statement."

"Is it enough?"

"For a warrant?" Scalia mulled that one over for a moment. "Probably not. But it might be enough for a look see."

"Who knows what will find once we're in there."

"Right."

Dustin "Sunflower" Cantwell was sitting behind the counter of the store, doing paperwork when Scalia and Miller walked in. He was momentarily stunned by the sight of Scalia in his black uniform coming down the stairs to the floor of the shop. The two customers who were checking out pipes in the display cases froze. Cantwell figured it was just another roust.

Scalia and Miller smelled marijuana and lots of it. The whole store reeked of it.

"Where are the kids?" Miller demanded.

"What?" said Cantwell.

"The kids that were in here." Miller didn't wait for an answer. He headed towards the back of the long, narrow basement to look for the kids he'd seen enter, now almost 20 to 25 minutes ago. Scalia ordered the two customers against the wall and then searched them. He found a small quantity of marijuana in the backpack of one of them.

Miller returned to the front of the store empty-handed.

"I think they've left."

Miller and Scalia were standing there, not quite sure what to do next, when Alan Middlemiss came down the stairs.

"What the fuck is going on here?"

Miller grabbed Middlemiss while Scalia searched his pockets.

"This is illegal — you guys can't do this," he protested.

"What is this?" Scalia held up a small baggie.

"Not much," said Middlemiss.

Scalia sniffed it. "Bingo."

"OK, you're done," said Miller. Scalia cuffed him and brought him up the stairs and into the unmarked car now parked in the alley.

"Everybody else out." Miller ushered the two customers and Cantwell out into the street and then went back inside. Scalia told one customer to expect a possession summons and headed inside the store.

53

Inside the cop car, Middlemiss yelled at Cantwell, "Look inside! Look through the window and see what they're doing."

Cantwell peered through the dirty, partially covered window and saw Scalia and Miller milling around the store. He banged on the window.

"Hey," he yelled. "You can't search in there."

Scalia spotted him and came outside.

"We found a baggie of dope in there."

"Where?"

"On the counter."

"Bullshit."

Scalia waves him off and turns to his car. "I'm going to get a warrant." He opened the rear car door and let Middlemiss out.

"We'll be back for both you guys in a bit." He started up the car and drove off. Miller came out of the store and stood by the door.

"Can we go back in now?" asked Cantwell.

"No. We're getting a warrant and then it will be a while."

"You're busting us?"

"That's right."

Here's the grounds for belief Scalia submitted for the search warrant:

> 1. On October 10th, 1997, Sgt. Scalia received information from a source that he had witnessed transactions between youths and the operators of the Holy Smoke Culture Shop. The source felt that the proprietors were selling drugs, as the transactions were seen and a high volume of traffic to and from the store [sic]. The source reports that there have been numerous youths congregating at the Holy Smoke during the past months, before school, at noon hour and after school on a consistent basis.
>
> 2. The Holy Smoke Culture Shop is a store devoted to the sale of drug paraphernalia, specifically cannabis products, and the promotion of smoking marijuana and its derivatives.
>
> 3. The proprietors of the Holy Smoke Culture Shop openly advocate the repeal of Canadian drug laws pertaining to cannabis.
>
> 4. Subsequent to the initial information obtained, on October 15, 1997, Sgt Scalia received information that more than one person was smoking marijuana in the Holy Smoke Culture Shop with the consent of the owner.

5. At 1215 hours, October 15, 1997, Sgt. Scalia and Det. Miller attended the Holy Smoke Culture Shop at 422 Herridge Lane, Nelson BC. The store was open to the public and two customers were present at that time. Immediately upon entry, both officers noted a heavy smell of marijuana smoke in the premise. Det. Miller subsequently noted a bag of marijuana (bud) lying in plain view on the counter used by employees. One of the proprietors, Dustin Sunflower Cantwell, was at the counter when officers entered the store.

6. One of the stores proprietors, Alan Stewart Middlemiss, entered the store and was arrested by Det. Miller. He was searched and found to be in personal possession of a small quantity of cannabis.

7. The granting of a warrant to search will enable lawful seizure of the marijuana seen within the premise and any other controlled substances, precursors, property or things on the premise.

55

Returning to the store, a crowd had begun to gather, drawn by the squad car in front of the infamous shop. The third owner of the store, Paul DeFelice had shown up and so had Const. Bill Clay, the Drug Awareness Officer for the RCMP. Clay had been called to provide some extra security to aid in the search when it happened. Clay was an expert in drug operations and worked closely with the NCP when needed.

At the moment, however, he was engaged in semi-friendly debate with DeFelice on the medical benefits of marijuana. Clay, a good-natured guy who enjoyed the respect of cops and druggies, was incredulous.

"So you're telling me that marijuana smoke isn't bad for you?"

"The benefits of marijuana as a medicine have been documented for thousands of years," DeFelice shot back.

"Yeah, but smoke is bad. It's bad for your lungs, respiratory system, the whole thing. So even if there are good things about it, and I'm not saying that there are, getting it into your body is damaging it," he said.

"But—"

"Well, isn't it bad for you?"

This circular debate would have continued had Middlemiss not come up to Clay and handed him a good-sized marijuana bud.

"Now are you going to arrest me? For that small amount?" he said defiantly.

Clay considered the bud a moment then threw it through a sewer grate in the alley.

"I tell you what Alan, you take me to your stash and then we'll talk about busting you, how's that? It seems to me you've got enough trouble on your hands as it is today," Clay said.

"It's you guys that are going to have the trouble. This is a great day for us. We're going to take this case all the way to the Supreme Court and get marijuana legalized. This day will be looked back on as a seminal event in the history of pot," Middlemiss pronounced.

"Sure kid," Clay chuckled.

Scalia served the warrant on Middlemiss, then he, Miller, and two other cops tore the place apart. They found what they were looking for: dope, 76 grams of it, some of it packaged in little baggies labeled with 1/4 and 1/8 labels. They found cash. They found 24 grams of magic mushrooms, in 5 gram packages. They found bongs and pipes and all kinds of other drug paraphernalia. And they took pictures: pictures of drug posters, pictures of bongs, pictures of the walls — it was one big Kodak moment.

The cops confiscated everything, carrying out boxes full of stuff. Their search took and two and a half hours and when it was done, the cops were confident that they had what they needed to shut Holy Smoke forever.

57

7

Middlemiss

*I*n a moment that can only be looked back on with irony, Alan Stewart Middlemiss, proprietor of the Holy Smoke Culture Shop in Nelson, was introduced to marijuana by a cop.

He hadn't done any drugs in grade school in the Toronto suburb of Oshawa, Ontario, having had exposure to the more traditional cigarettes and alcohol rather than cannabis-related substances. Then a community police officer came in to tell his class about the ills of drugs, particularly weed.

"I thought to myself, what the hell are they so afraid of?"

He first smoked up in 1985 when he was 16 years old, taking a little toke with his older sisters. Though he enjoyed the experience of being high, marijuana helped him develop a connection with parts of the natural world that were otherwise difficult to grasp.

"I had an environmental outlook and I thought that cannabis helped keep me earthy when I was living in this big, dirty city right outside Toronto," he says.

In the working class environment that was Oshawa, Middlemiss felt isolated from the crowd wearing Kodiak boots and lumber jackets, much as DeFelice did growing up in Sudbury fifteen years before. Many of Alan's experiences were similar as well.

"I'd go outside at a party and smoke a joint and come back in and not drink. I'd see people puking and fighting and generally being assholes. I found that people that I was with when I was smoking pot would be talking about the world, current events, politics, trading ideas. When I was drunk it was all sexual innuendo leading to fighting,"

Following high school, Middlemiss headed to Toronto and worked a variety of odd jobs, not finding anything of particular interest. One day he came across a promotional brochure for B.C. "I saw a pamphlet that said 'Super Natural British Columbia' and I thought I'd see how super natural it was, so I moved to Vancouver."

60

Middlemiss got involved in a variety of environmental issues while on the coast and smoked marijuana steadily while working in construction.

"I smoked every day for 15 years and I've held steady jobs in the trades. It doesn't slow down my productivity or make me lethargic like it's been portrayed in the media. I've seen people smoking all day, every day, as much as they can and they're still not bad people," he says.

Involved in the marijuana subculture as well, Middlemiss met DeFelice in 1990 at the Grateful Dead show in Hamilton.

At Paul's urging, Alan came to Nelson and found the community and environment he had been searching for all these years.

"As soon as I saw the place, I fell in love with it," he says.

Living with his wife and starting a family, it seemed to Middlemiss that everyone around him was growing marijuana.

"My wife and I lived all over the Nelson area — from Queen's Bay, Kaslo, Balfour, South Slocan, Krestova — and everywhere we went it seemed that one out of every two people were growing. They were older, younger —it didn't matter. It wasn't anything like you see on TV or in magazines, the whole party scene – it wasn't anything like that. It's very natural, it's just part of the garden, no big deal," he says.

He started growing, mostly for his own personal use and began to get involved in the fight to decriminalize marijuana. It was that struggle that lead to his involvement with Holy Smoke.

"We decided that we wanted to take it to a new level of education. It isn't legalization we are interested in, it is decriminalization. We want binding laws that an adult that is in possession of a certain amount of cannabis is not considered a dealer. It can't be proven that possession of cannabis does harm to others in any way. Whether it does harm to one's self is debatable, but the premise of a crime is doing harm someone else.

"We thought the best thing to do was to be up front about what we were doing. Yes I am an adult. Yes I smoke cannabis. People shouldn't be afraid," he says.

Middlemiss says when he, Paul and Dustin first started the store there was some backlash from the usual suspects — cops, religious groups, parents — but also from some less predictable sources: commercial growers.

"They were upset with us. They thought because we were taking such a public stance we were attracting unnecessary attention to the entire scene. They wouldn't have anything to do with us.

"That's fine. We wanted to be a voice for the local, non-commercial cannabis community," he says. "People are accepting that this is a part of Nelson that you can't deny. We made it legitimate, in a sense."

The only aspect of marijuana that Middlemiss struggles with is how to deal with his children, now five and eight years of age.

"I don't talk to my kids about pot. There was this huge bust on the news one day and my daughter said 'Daddy, marijuana is bad.' I said, 'Okay, fair enough,' and I basically changed the subject because she'll make up her own mind. It's an adult issue."

Like many others in the community, Middlemiss sees marijuana as part of his religious outlook on life. "Smoking cannabis is not a recreational thing, it's a deep, meaningful, spiritual thing."

He feels the negative images of the Nelson dope smoking community — and of Holy Smoke in particular — promoted by police and politicians is a fallacy.

"Our premise from the beginning has been that we are decent people and that all the people we deal with are decent people. We've proven that."

✳ ✳ ✳

The wheels of justice turn slowly, and that wasn't good enough for Scalia and the NCP. They wanted Holy Smoke shut down *now*. So Scalia went down to city hall and had a chat with the city clerk and building inspector to tell them what the police had found. The city clerk — the wife of an NCP officer — and the building inspector in turn had a chat with Mayor Exner, and his responce was clear: shut them down. The city revoked the business license for the Holy Smoke Culture Shop that afternoon. The hope was that with no business license, the boys would simply pack up their dope tent and go back whence they came.

It kept the store shut for exactly five days. The Holy Smoke owners got lawyers, and their advice was also pretty clear: they can't shut you down, or revoke your license without a hearing. And being charged with a crime (which had yet to happen) wasn't enough to revoke the license at any rate: only a criminal conviction, evidence that the store was being used for illegal means, was grounds for pulling the business license. So Holy Smoke stayed open for now.

Gary Exner, a conservative accountant with two small children of his own was nonetheless pleased with the developments. He saw Holy Smoke as a blemish on his law-abiding town. He realized, however, that he couldn't pull the license simply because he thought Cantwell, DeFelice and Middlemiss were elements of the community he didn't like. He found a more creative solution: they were in violation of their business license because they allowed minors under the age of 16 to smoke in the store — not necessarily dope, but just smoking period.

Council argued behind closed doors — conservatives advocating for immediate closure, liberals wanting the justice system to run its course. They got legal counsel. Their advice: wait for a conviction. The city rescinded its suspension of Holy Smoke's business license two weeks after issuing it. It mattered little, as the store had stayed open anyway.

But this whole business license deal had given Mayor Exner some new ideas about how he might be able to get rid of this problem all by himself.

In the early part of December 1997, Nelson city council unveiled a new business license fee structure. Perhaps "unveil" is the wrong word; "sprung" is a better word, considering nobody — from the little retailers on Baker Street to the captains of industry that had worked so hard to elect Gary Exner a year before — knew anything about it.

The new system was surprisingly democratic in structure. It changed the flat $100 fee that every business paid to a sliding scale that charged businesses with larger retail spaces or greater revenue more. So the small shops got a marginal increase, from $100 to $120, but big banks went from paying $100 to $1000, as did the huge Wal-Mart in the mall. Paying fees for hotels and real estate agencies — the majority of which were owned by long-time Nelson families and Exner supporters — went from $100 to around $500 or $600.

Needless to say, the business community went ballistic. Though the new system was on its face far more fair, these businesses didn't like having there license fees cranked 500 per cent overnight with no warning by a guy who they'd stuck their necks out for. Many felt Mayor Exner had screwed them.

But that wasn't even the best part. City council, in its infinite wisdom, had cranked Holy Smoke's business license fee to the $1000 max. Holy Smoke, all 700 square feet of basement space of it, was now paying as much for its business license as Wal-Mart, the CIBC and the Bank of Montreal. Lofty company indeed.

64

The city had specifically created a new business license category for shops selling "water pipes, hooka pipes or bong pipes" and charged those businesses $1000. The funny thing was that that category encompassed only one business in Nelson: Holy Smoke.

Cantwell, DeFelice and Middlemiss were back on their soap box for marijuana decriminalization. Business was picking up thanks to all the free advertising the bust and now the license fee debacle had created. The Holy Smoke situation was again the topic of coffee house conversation.

And they had picked up some new allies — or at least the sympathy of some folks. Even if the general public was willing to believe that Holy Smoke was a device of the doped-up, many were uncomfortable with the idea of a government creating laws that specifically targeted one business. The big city refugees were generally more liberal and more politically vocal than the long-time Nelsonites.

The Nelson-lifers were too pissed at Mayor Exner about their own business license problems to worry about the dope fiends. And these were guys that Exner typically called on for support. "Well," he'd usually say, "I've had dozens of calls supporting our decision." His cronies were calling alright, but it wasn't to congratulate him for sticking it to Holy Smoke. They were calling to rip him a new one for boosting their business licenses 500 per cent.

The issue even got the attention of media beyond Nelson. Nelson already had a reputation for some pretty draconian bylaws. The summer before, the town city council had passed a bylaw banning dogs in the downtown core, leashes or not, because of complaints, they said, about hippies letting their dogs run loose on Baker Street, fighting, shitting and humping everywhere. There was also a law banning hackey-sack playing downtown after one too many senior citizens got hoofed on the way to the bank. And no more bongo drum playing, that was banned too. Sheriff Exner was cleansing Dodge City of the Gang that couldn't smoke straight.

But this latest bylaw was just too much to take. CBC Radio did an interview with Exner and Middlemiss, where Exner mentioned the word "undesirables" as in, we are trying to rid our community of "undesirables." The tourist operators, long selling this town as a creative, eclectic, artistic place to visit, did a collective head slap.

Mayor Exner's reasoning was simple and two-fold. First, he argued, businesses like Holy Smoke cost the city more money because of the increased costs of policing and enforcement. He was, of course, referring to the bust just two months earlier. But that theory had some obvious holes. The local bars and night clubs, which were now paying $500 for business licenses, required astronomically more policing than Holy Smoke did. Every Friday and Saturday night there were drunk people wandering around, starting fights just after closing time — the normal bar schtick. There were two cruisers and four officers on duty during the evenings, versus one cruiser during the day, for the express reason that the freaks came out to drink and break stuff after dark. And what about convenience stores? Shoplifting, cigarette selling — why weren't their taxes sky high?

Secondly, Exner did the same thing Scalia did when he wrote his memo to Chief Oak: he played the kid card.

"Those who sell or retail paraphernalia that is used for the illegal use of drugs, yes we have a problem with that because of the vulnerability of our youth. We're just trying to do everything in our power to stop that," Exner said.

"There is no other use for those pipes, they're not used in making wine or anything else … they're used for taking illegal drugs."

He was right of course. Those water bongs and ornate glass pipes on sale at the Holy Smoke Culture Shop weren't intended for anything else except getting high as kite on a windy day. The problem was the section of the Criminal Code outlawing their sale has been struck down.

And as usual, the Holy Smokers denied the charge that they were selling anything to anyone under the age of 18, no matter what the police or the city said. As they pointed out, selling drug kits to kiddies was the fastest way to lose public support and get rail-roaded out of town.

"The accusation that we allowed people under the age of 18 to smoke on the premises has absolutely no backing, no meat," Middlemiss said in October, just after the bust. "We never allowed anyone under the age of 18 to smoke there, let alone buy smoking accessories."

Just as the business license issue got going, the Crown Attorney brought charges against Cantwell, Dustin Sunflower;

Middlemiss, Alan Stewart, and DeFelice, Paul Stephen. The charges were the same for all three:

> Count #1: on or about October 15, 1997 at or near British Columbia, did unlawfully possess a controlled substance, to wit: Psilocin. Contrary to Sec 4(1) of the Controlled Drugs and Substances Act.

> Count #2: on or about October 15, 1997 at or near British Columbia, did unlawfully possess a controlled substance, to wit: Psilocin, for the purpose of trafficking. Contrary to Sec 5(2) of the Controlled Drugs and Substances Act.

> Count #3: on or about October 15, 1997 at or near British Columbia, did unlawfully posses a controlled substance, to wit: Cannabis Marijuana in an amount greater than thirty grams, Contrary to Sec 4(1) of the Controlled Drugs and Substances Act.

> Count #4: on or about October 15, 1997 at or near British Columbia, did unlawfully posses a controlled substance, to wit: Cannabis Marijuana in an amount not exceeding three kilograms, for the purpose of trafficking, Contrary to Sec 5(1) of the Controlled Drugs and Substances Act.

67

The translation: simple possession of magic mushrooms, as well as possession of mushrooms with the intent to sell; simple possession of about $300 worth of dope, and possession of less than three keys of dope intending to sell it.

If convicted, DeFelice, Middlemiss and Cantwell faced probation and a fine.

But that wasn't really the point: if these fellas were convicted of possession or intent to sell drugs in the Holy Smoke Culture Shop, the city would have the legal grounds they needed to pull their business license — The same business license were being asked to pay 1000 bucks for — and close the shop forever..

The laying of charges helped sway the public relations battle back towards the mayor: Remember folks, these people are drug dealers selling to our kids. On the heels of the CBC Radio interview about "undesirables" and the body blows he was taking about his harsh tactics, the charges were a reaffirmation of his point: these people were criminals that had to be stopped. The business license fiasco and laying of charges in the drug bust were not, however, in anyway related — it was just good timing.

"It's an absolute coincidence," Chief Oak said. "The exhibits had to be sent away for analysis, Crown Counsel's approval had to be received, so there is absolutely no link between the two."

Either way, the owners of the Holy Smoke Culture Shop now had two separate fights on their hands: one against the city for unfairly boosting their business license, and one against the NCP for drug charges. The shop's owners seemed resolute and fairly confident, at least publicly.

"Our lawyers have looked into this and shown us some case law where municipalities are not supposed to use business licenses as a prohibitory measure against businesses. So if the courts agree that the city passed this bylaw to try and prohibit us from doing business, then we may have a case against them," DeFelice said.

Middlemiss was equally optimistic they could beat the drug rap.

"I'm very confident that at the same time as us being exonerated, that we will aid in the cannabis laws in Canada being changed," he said.

The mayor for his part was unconcerned about the threat of a lawsuit.

"Almost anything and everything is possible," he said. "We're not about to back down."

Nobody was. It was going to be left to the courts to decide the fate of the Holy Smoke Culture Shop.

The business license fee hike was easier of the two problems to deal with: the Holy Smoke owners simply didn't pay the full balance. They paid $120 — the same amount other businesses of their size were paying. Though it put them in contradiction of civic bylaws, there was no immediate way for the city to summarily close Holy Smoke without going to court — which is where Holy Smoke planned to fight the fee hike as discriminatory.

And at the time the City of Nelson had its plate full of court cases. From 1996 to 1999 the City of Nelson went to court over everything from the building of a new hotel, to an improper zoning usage, to leaky condos, to the legality of parking tickets, to accusations of conflict of interest around the council table. They even had a B.C. Human Rights tribunal case brought by a female city worker over pornography in the workplace. The city of Nelson was spending a lot of money on legal fees. It was a litigious time, and they'd get to Holy Smoke in due course.

69

Holy Smoke also had some unexpected support. Several other businesses were fighting their new business licenses as well. In the irony of ironies, a few of these businesses were owned by the some of the most old school, conservative families in town. The dirty hippies and the Nelson-lifers united together against Mayor Gary Exner and the City of Nelson. It was beautiful.

The court case against Holy Smoke finally got rolling at the end of April 1998, as the three defendants entered "not guilty" pleas. The possession and trafficking of mushrooms charges had been dropped by the federal Crown prosecutor Rob Brown and the three now just faced simple possession charges. A deal was also offered: plead guilty to simple possession, get a fine and maybe a little probation.

The three mulled over the offer. It would be less expensive, considering DeFelice and Cantwell had retained lawyers and they weren't cheap. There would be no personal consequence. But the store would be in jeopardy. There was little question the city would use the criminal convictions as fodder to try and deny them a business license. Everything they'd worked for would be gone and the cops and Exner would win. It wasn't very appealing.

Not to mention the fact there was a point to be proved here and a soapbox from which to trumpet their views. The case was surely to get some kick-ass press and, win or lose, it would be a chance to speak out for what they believed in. This was their chance to contribute something substantial to the fight.

Besides, the lawyers were optimistic the case could be won. There were, they said, major problems with the search warrant and with a little luck, the three could get off completely. Though the plan had initially been to use the case as an indictment of the cannabis laws in Canada and an examination of dope smoking as an issue of religious and personal freedom, by the time the case got to court that strategy had started to change. DeFelice's lawyer, Don Skogstad, was a Charter of Rights fanatic, and he thought he had a case that the search warrant was illegally obtained. It wasn't as good as saying dope laws were wrong, but putting the cops and their methods on trial was also appealing. The case was held over until September.

In the meantime, the city finally got around to suing Holy Smoke and all the other businesses for not paying their business license fee. In July the City of Nelson applied in small claims court to have the businesses cough up. The businesses banded together and got legal counsel from lawyer Blair Suffredine. He advised them to try and get the case moved to Supreme Court and then to argue that the fees were unfairly raised. The prime example: Holy Smoke. Not that the Holy Smokers weren't super keen to be incurring more legal fees but they were perfectly comfortable letting Suffredine use their good name to try his case on behalf of other merchants and real estate agents..

Suffredine, never shy with the press, did some mighty grandstanding. He suggested publicly that a victory in court could mean the city would be forced to refund all the business license fee for 1998. There was hand-wringing going on at city hall. Perhaps there was a way to settle this once and for all.

Two things of interest happened while the Holy Smokers were awaiting trial. The first was Ross Rebagliati's Olympic snowboarding victory in February of 1998 and the ensuing weirdness surrounding his positive test for marijuana. (As you may recall, Rebagliati's gold medal was rescinded following his positive test results. Arguments ensued over the validity of the test and whether marijuana was a banned substance under Olympic rules. After an appeal, Rebagliati got his gold medal back.)

For Nelson, this event was a momentous occasion, as it is both a snowboarding and dope smoking Mecca. There were several people in town who knew Rebagliati. Lumpy Leidel, the man that Ross tearily dedicated his run to, had been killed in an avalanche along with six others just outside of Nelson a month before the Olympics.

Holy Smoke jumped right on the bandwagon, printing up T-shirts that featured a snowboarder over a Canadian flag that had a cannabis leaf instead of a maple. The caption read "Just say... Naga no." It was a play on Nagano, Japan where the Olympics were held and the infamous "Just Say No" anti-drug campaign of the Reagan era. These T-shirts were very popular and the *Daily News* did a story on them and the debate that swirled around Rebagliati. The story featured a front page photo, taken in Holy Smoke, of a guy wearing a toque, sunglasses, one of the T-shirts and smoking a huge spliff.

The Holy Smokers used the occasion to promote the idea that it was possible for a dope smoker to do anything, including win a gold medal. The idea that Rebagliati tested positive for dope because of second-hand smoke is laughable to anyone who has ever been to Whistler, where he trained, or knows anything about the culture there. (Which is a whole other book entirely.)

But think back — wasn't it a bit strange to see Prime Minister Jean Chretien and all these other high profile Canadian politicians standing up for "Fatty" Rebagliati? The guy became an overnight sensation, a media darling and corporate spokesperson, entirely because he had tested positive for bud. Considering how other athletes, such as sprinter Ben Johnson, have been vilified for testing positive for drugs in this country, it was unusual that the country actually treated Rebagliati like a hero. The message seemed to be: it's only dope.

For some it was yet another sign of society's growing ambivalence toward marijuana laws. For others it was yet another sign of the impending apocalypse.

The other strange event that kept Holy Smoke in the news was their assertion in March of 1998 that they were now the Holy Smoke Mission of God. It seems that the owners of Holy Smoke had formed a loose affiliation with the Church of the Universe, an Ontario-based group of aging hippies that claimed smoking dope was tenet of their religious beliefs (along with walking around naked), and that their arrest by Ontario Provincial Police violated their Constitutional Right to religious freedom.

Except no one, including the Holy Smokers seemed to know what their "religious freedom" meant.

"I'm sure not sure what it entitles us to as an organization," Cantwell told the *Daily News*. "If we're a church, there may be a way to bypass having a business license."

It was an interesting ploy, but one the city shot down in a hurry. If they were truly serious about being a church, came the city's response, they were in the wrong zoning and would have apply for a different zoning or relocate. Whoops.

The mayor took the opportunity to land a solid blow: "Smoking marijuana is against the law and breaking the law doesn't seem to be … a very Christian thing to do."

The Holy Smokers never mentioned it again.

73

8

The Dope Swami

Dustin "Sunflower" Cantwell is sitting in a Nelson restaurant eating a tofu scramble and talking marijuana philosphy between bites. One of the founding owners of the Holy Smoke Culture Shop, he is by far the most existential of the three. Despite the fact that the restaurant is three-quarters full with mid-morning traffic, Cantwell expresses his views on marijuana without lowering his voice or looking around to see if anyone's listening. With his big, bushy beard and white skullcap, he stands out slightly, but nobody takes notice — just two guys talking about marijuana, ho hum. His personal philosophy best exemplifies the Holy Smoke perspective so here is Sunflower in conversation.

How do you define yourself?

I believe in exploring all the parts of life. That you don't have just one thing that you do: I want it all — music, poetry, writing, art. A lot of the people in this area are lovers of life; we want to grow beautiful gardens, make music, shake our butts to reggae, we want to live. That's how I want to live my life, that I'm part of a glorious tale and I want my part to be exciting.

So how does marijuana fit into that?
For me, it's not a recreational thing. I'm not into Holy Smoke because I'm a big pot smoker, like "Whoo bong hits, let's do it up! Party!" That's not the reason that we have to make a stand and fight for our rights. This has to do with spirituality, autonomy over one's body, autonomy over one's spirit. The state can have laws that protect you from harm, but if there is no harm, the state should never intercede in your life. But our government, the laws of men have decided that smoking cannabis is subject to criminal prosecution, even though there is no victim. For me, when I smoke cannabis it's a direct link between me and God or prayer. The smoke enters me, close to my energy, my organs and into that smoke I translate my being and I exhale that into the air as a prayer. For somebody to tell me that I can't do that, that I can't express my belief in the world in that way, is ridiculous. The whole argument that a plant can be illegal is absurd. And when I had my son I wanted to make sure this place that I'm bringing him into is good and wholesome and that he never has to go through the same bullshit that I had to go through. If there's something unjust I want to work against it so that when he matures that injustice won't be there for him to brunt.

So how did you get into marijuana?
When I moved to this area I started growing cannabis, heading up the mountain with backpacks and slowly growing the plant, get-

ting to know how seeds work — always organic. It was never huge harvests but enough that I began to make a communion with the plant. I began to realize that this plant tied in with my spirituality so I was actually growing my sacrament. All of a sudden it became a whole different thing. Instead of buying it in a baggie, I was growing it and spending time with the plant and seeing the glorious creation of god. The cannabis plant when it's full grown is six or seven feet high, its leaves waving at you, it's a spectacle. It was like making your own wine for sacrament in church. I found plants grown organically and with love, the high they produced was more of a high than the buds that were grown indoors under lamps for money. It became something more. You weren't just going to sell off what you had just grown, because money didn't cover it, it was priceless.

Did you sell it?
Nope.

Never sold it?
No. I usually gave it away, or in the Kootenays it was the original barter. It was the hemp standard: one gram equals ten dollars equals one hour of work.

Are there dealers in the community?
So many people grow, there is no real need for a street-level dealer, I'll tell you that right now. If you aren't growing it yourself or don't know a buddy or a neighbor that is growing it... you know what I'm saying? That's why when people say "Does Holy Smoke sell cannabis?", if they're coming to me in the most heated-out store of all time to find buds, they're in trouble. There's nothing I can do.

Hard to grasp a place without dealers.

I know, I used to have to do it all the time. We used to call it "the hunt" because you'd have to lurk in alleys and ask around and it might take hours or days to find a bag of bud. Here in Nelson it's like, "popcorn, peanuts, cannabis."

But there is an industry here.
Definitely. I mean in the 1980s this community was going down, the university closed, KFP shut down. I mean, what industry is there here really? Not much, but people are growing bud and that's why we survived. There's an alternative economy here that is worth hundreds of millions of dollars tax free, injected right into the economy. And when small, folksy people make money off pot, they don't go and buy fancy cars, go swing in the clubs and fly in jets. They buy houses, they feed their kids, they make their lives better and they try to participate in the community more.

But how does that work?
SUNFLOWER: Everybody grows. So when you go to get your car fixed, you say, here's an eighth, so slice off some of the charge. Or I need a new roof, here's a couple ounces. Or you've got a buddy in Ontario who can't get bud, but they're family but you're going out on a visit so you bring an ounce. It's not the dealer concept, it just makes it so you can edge things off. The other thing is, everybody smokes it so you're saving your money by not having to buy it.

So if dope is so great why is it illegal?
It gets back to consciousness. There's two forms of society, dominator and non-dominator. A non-dominator society is where people function together, cooperate. There's no need to rule people. But because we've grown up in a warring society, we've grown up in a dominator society. You can see it all around us.

The government controls us, the army dominates. The ideal dominator drug is alcohol. Dominator mentality is in the animal part of the brain, the stupid part of your brain, which is the part the alcohol affects. Makes people perfect candidates to be dominated. You would rarely need peace officers if alcohol was gone. Non-dominator drugs are like cannabis, mushrooms, where you don't feel the need to dominate, you're not trying to jump on women, you know what I mean? Now marijuana affects the higher part of your brain, it makes you relaxed, even creative. So our dominator-based society doesn't want non-dominator drugs because it strikes at the very root of what they're trying to do. Tied in there is consciousness. Dominator society controls everything: they control food, cars, sex, advertising, how buildings are built, all this physical realm stuff. They have complete control: economics, politics, education, military. The only realm they don't have control over is our consciousness, spirituality, dimensional travel, the very essence of ourselves. There's many bandwidths of reality and our little bandwidth is the horse-flesh bandwidth; all the other bandwidths stretch out from that point. Within every person is an unexplored realm, deeper and more glorious than this realm.

79

And marijuana helps you get there?
Marijuana helps you break into those other realms. The dominators are afraid of what we will discover, that within in our minds there is a power that can free us. So any drugs that help us discover those realms have to be excluded because if people discover this potential within them, it will be all over. So that's why cannabis is banned. Our renaissance will be when we discover our consciousness.

So how do you make this a reality? Decriminalization? Legalization?

Legalization means the government is in control of it. I don't like that idea. Anytime the government is in charge of something they screw it up. They're in control of alcohol and they sell this swill water. Same with tobacco. We could have naturally papered, organically grown tobacco and it wouldn't be a problem. If cannabis were to fall into their hands all we'd get is chemically grown, genetically engineered swag. Then there's decriminalization so it's not illegal to do it. Well, that opens it up to groups to make money and generate corruption and make things worse. I don't like that idea either. So the one we've come to work toward is regulation, where nobody's in charge of it but there's a regulating body that insures potency, costs, taxes.

Would people still be able to grow it?
Absolutely. If you let people grow like 30 plants a year, you would see the crime element virtually disappear because most people only need 1/4 pound a year to smoke. Like myself, I get chided continuously because I'm the flyweight of Holy Smoke.

Now what about the kids? Every time Holy Smoke comes up the police and Gary Exner bring up the kids...
I do so much drug counseling at Holy Smoke I almost think that's ridiculous. I have kids coming in there from every spectrum—

Why are they asking you?
Because they want the truth and they're not getting it from school, or the cops or their parents. No one ever talks to kids truthfully about marijuana, or mushrooms or LSD. Hell, there's a whole realm of drugs I haven't even tried, that I can't even tell them about, like methamphetamine, MDMA — I'm still a generation behind.

So what to do you tell a kid about pot?

I always assume they're going to do it, because if you tell them not to do it just makes them want to do it more. So then I try and set a principle of harm reduction. What you're going to smoke, do you know where you're getting it from, is it organic? Do you have the proper things to smoke it with? Then there's the principle of set and setting. What's your mind-set, what are you thinking? You don't want to go to a bar angry at your girlfriend, broken-hearted or anything. You want to be clean-minded. Then there's setting, the physical environment. I always recommend they do it in nature, not in a bar or a party. This concrete, man-made world is not conducive to the higher realms. I just try and eliminate harm.

There are people that would say that by telling teenagers this stuff, you're encouraging it.
I don't encourage, I just say if you're going to do it, do it safely. Discouraging kids never works, it's the forbidden fruit principle. It worked on me. All these people telling me not to do it, I had to try it because adults bullshit you all the time. You don't tend to believe them, so you have to try it for yourself. But if somebody gives me the honest truth, I'll do it when I'm ready. An educated kid won't make foolish mistakes. You never see a teenager dying of smoking cannabis, but I see all these kids dying of drinking and driving. I've seen mothers distraught over their daughters, plundered by drunken men. That doesn't happen to cannabis smokers. You don't lose your faculties, your sense of decency when you're smoking cannabis. If we're going to pick a legal drug let's pick a good one.

9

The Defenders:
Suffredine and Skogstad do the law thing

83

Caught in the middle between the cops and the crooks are the lawyers. With a lifestyle more similar to police officers than to the clients they are charged with defending, the criminal lawyers of Nelson walk a fine line between protecting the rights that protect us all and releasing the folks back into society that make people cross the street. Here's an up close look at criminal lawyer and accidental Holy Smoke defender Blair Suffredine and Holy Smoke trial lawyer Don Skogstad.

Blair Suffredine loves to win. He loves it. He explains it to his clients — some of them charged with the most heinous crimes a small town can generate — as the Golden Rules.

It started with his first major case as a budding criminal lawyer in Nelson in the early 1980s. He took a jury trial for a guy named Gord Stelter who was charged with robbing a local grocery store. The alleged facts were a couple of guys on a motorcycle had gone into the store and held it up at gunpoint. When they tried to get away, however, the motorcycle wouldn't start and they ran away. The police later picked up a groom and a best man from a local wedding and charged them with the crime, saying they had left the hall, robbed the grocery store and returned to the reception. Stelter was the best man.

The evidence against them was pretty good. The police had a confession and Stelter's girlfriend worked at the grocery store in question. Stelter and the groom had been doing serious cocaine for days before the wedding. When Stelter came to Suffredine a few weeks before the trial, the case looked like a real loser. But Suffredine figured there was little to lose in taking a case that nobody thought he could win. Besides, he had nothing more pressing on his plate.

It was a long and complicated jury trial that was well covered by the press. The Crown's case, however, fell apart when it came out that Stelter had suffered a serious leg injury a month before the crime was committed and had only gotten off crutches a few days before the robbery took place. The idea that he had somehow managed to sprint away from the crime scene was impossible. The jury acquitted.

Early in the case, however Suffredine says Stelter came to him, concerned that his lawyer didn't believe him.

"I told him, 'Look, you've got to understand the rules: the day I start believing you is the day I'm no good to you. I will not believe you, I won't even try. It's very important that I not believe you and that I not believe the Crown — I simply say, here's the evidence, here's a legal defense we can raise. I win for me, not for you. I care about me not you, because it matters to me that I win.'

"He said: 'I like these rules.' From then on I made sure that anybody that came in understood the Golden Rules."

In addition to spawning the Golden Rules, Stelter's case had another benefit. According to Suffredine, the *Nelson Daily News* reporter missed the crucial day of the trial, and when the verdict was reported it looked like Suffredine performed some kind of legal miracle: he'd won a can't-miss loser. His reputation for taking the impossible cases — and occasionally winning them — was born.

Suffredine himself was born in Saskatoon in 1951 but his parents moved to Regina in 1953. Dad was a customs broker, helping people import and export commercial goods. Suffredine's father had aspired to university but missed out because he grew up during the war years. Instead he traveled, seeing Europe for free while riding a troop train between battles. His father had seen friends who'd gone to school do much better than he did, and there was a great deal of pressure on young Blair to get an education.

85

"Back in those days a university degree opened up a lot of doors that weren't open for a guy like my father that only had grade nine. He was adamant that he would pay and we would go. It didn't matter how hard it was to raise the money," Suffredine says.

He enrolled in the Commerce program at the University of Saskatchewan in Regina, but kept the option of law school open, taking law courses as his electives.

When it came to article, Suffredine looked hard for a place he would enjoy. A firm in Kamloops turned him down and a large Calgary firm with marble floors gave Suffredine the heebie-jeebies. So Suffredine applied to Nelson lawyer Stuart Enderton. But Enderton told him he didn't need anyone, having just hired a student. However when the student didn't show up, Enderton went to Regina to recruit another. Suffredine convinced him to hire a kid who actually wanted to come to Nelson.

Suffredine wanted a small community and he wanted to ski. He'd been on several field trips while in university and — like Paul DeFelice — wanted to go to a place where he could find some serious powder.

"In Regina, people seemed to work all week so they could go to the beach on the weekend — and it wasn't much of a beach. Why would you work, work, work just so you could drive an hour each way to the lake?" he says.

Suffredine wanted to go some place where he could buy a place on the lake, ski within a reasonable distance and not have to work all the time to be able to do that.

He arrived in Nelson in 1974, when he was 22 years old. He ended up being partners with Stuart Enderton and then in 1983, when Enderton was appointed as provincial court judge, Suffredine bought him out and just carried on. This is the first and only job he's ever had.

86

Suffredine had not intended to practice criminal law. He excelled — and enjoyed — the scintillating specialty of tax law. But Enderton had been a litigator who loved the courtroom and he passed that love on to Suffredine. It was, he says, "like learning Shakespeare from a English professor who loves it." Enderton made criminal law fun.

Suffredine's practice is mostly criminal law but also includes contract disputes, real estate and other civil matters. He tries to stay away from divorce and custody battles because he takes it home with him. While there isn't enough criminal law in a small town to just do court work, there's little question that's where Suffredine's enthusiasm is greatest. He is able to defend those charged with the most dastardly crimes because he feels there is a great importance to his role. Suffredine has defended the last two murder cases in a small town that averages one every four or five years.

"When people are charged, the whole philosophy of criminal law is, don't judge them, they've got somebody to do that. I'm there to put forward whatever legitimate defense they have or, if they have absolutely none, to see what I can do to get them the best deal I can.

"There are a certain amount of tactics that come into play. You don't really want to run a criminal defense if you just know that it's hopeless. But on the other hand, often there are good potential defenses there."

The creativity in finding a defense, says Suffredine, is second on his happy list — after winning.

While Suffredine has enjoyed success in the courtroom he has been less successful as a politician. He has run for the federal seat twice, in 1993 and again in 1997, both times as Progressive Conservative.

When he first came to Nelson, Suffredine was signed up for the Conservatives by Enderton.

"While I was doing my articling there was an election going on and he said, Come with me you're going to come and help. He didn't give me any choice," Suffredine says.

As time went on he became more and more involved. In 1992 his dad, an avid political participant who had been encouraging his son to run for office, passed away. In the spring of 1993 a friend of Suffredine's tried to get him to run for the Conservatives. The problem, however, was that Suffredine hated PC Leader Mulroney (though he liked cabinet minister John Crosbie), so he said if Mulroney quits, I'll run – never suspecting Mulroney would do just that the very next week.

Suffredine lost that election, to Reform Party candidate Jim Gouk, who would also beat Suffredine in the rematch. The second time around, however, Suffredine's criminal lawyer instincts — and his overwhelming desire to win — would get the best of him.

During the campaign, Suffredine dug up evidence that Gouk had written to the makers of Tylenol — on his MP stationary no less — proposing that they feature him in a commercial. He even laid out the premise: Jim Gouk was an air traffic controller for blah blah years and he used to get terrible-ass headaches, for which he took Tylenol. Then Jim got elected to parliament and "now he gives the Liberals headaches," chortle, chortle, ha ha ha. Pretty stupid and pretty harmless, except Gouk had used parliamentary letterhead, an obvious breach of ethics. Somehow Suffredine got wind of this, got the letter and leaked it to the *Daily News* and proceeded to milk it to death as evidence of what a bad, unethical toad Jim Gouk was.

Gouk's a lot of things, but he's not unethical. He just made a stupid mistake for which he was immediately contrite. Suffredine, criminal attorney that he is, wouldn't let it drop, and in the end the voters of West Kootenay-Okanagan liked the mudslinging politics less than Gouk's boneheaded maneuver: Gouk was re-elected by a wide margin and Suffredine finished fifth behind the Green Party.

Suffredine has already announced he will seek the Liberal nomination in the next B.C. provincial election, the ultimate player in search of yet another game.

Don Skogstad was born in Kenora, Ont., in 1949 but grew up a prairie boy. His dad worked for the railway, directing the trains, and was transferred to Brandon, Manitoba A town of 30,000, just a few months after Don was born. Skogstad stayed in Brandon until he had finished his B.A. in economics. He left for Vancouver the day after graduation.

Skogstad was an admitted underachiever, scheduling classes only between 10:00 a.m. and 3:00 p.m. so he could sleep in but still be at the pool hall for the afternoon. Following graduation, he was still without direction and so, on a whim, he took the federal civil servant exam and was subsequently offered a job as a management trainee. He worked for the government for four years and sums up the experience easily: boring.

Though it took Skogstad a few years to realize it, he'd already been given a hint about his future direction. When he was 22 years old back in Brandon,, a friend of his was involved a dispute over severance pay. The friend had an appeal in front of the provincial labor board and, nervous about it, asked Skogstad to do it for him.

"I read over the law and I figured I could do it — what difference did it make, he would lose if he went himself anyway. I went through it, explained the arguments and goddamn it if we didn't win the thing. I thought to myself, 'Yeah, I could do this. I could do this,'" he says.

89

With that experience in mind, he wrote the law school admission test a few years later, the first academic endeavor he'd taken seriously. He got 97 per cent. So at 26, he enrolled at the University of British Columbia law school.

Skogstad was practicing criminal law by the second year of law school traveling on a regular basis to 222 Main St. in Vancouver, the biggest court in Canada. He got into it, was good at it. He articled with three criminal lawyers with vastly different styles: an anal preparedness nut, a guy who didn't read the files until he stepped into the courtroom, and a lawyer who came up with incredibly novel, creative defenses. The firm did half the murders in Vancouver the year Skogstad articled and, while assisting on some of those trials, he did 35 to 40 cases of his own. It was an exciting, high-stakes way to learn the law.

He briefly opened a practice in Vancouver with a friend from law school, but the prairie boy longed to get out of the city. He heard about a provincial prosecutors job in Nelson, applied and was hired. So in 1980, Skogstad and his soon-to-be wife moved to the Kootenays.

After two years in the Crown's office, however, Skogstad was getting worried about money. There was a wage freeze and he now had a young family to support. Additionally, he wanted to get experience in areas other than criminal law. Unfortunately, Skogstad's move to private practice coincided with the very public Nelson recession. He rented out the basement of his house, slowly built a practice and just hung on. He did every different kind of law imaginable.

Slowly, however, he was able to narrow his practice so that he was able to stick with what he was good at and what he enjoyed: court work.

He also developed a reputation as a specialist in marijuana cases, particularly grow-ops, to the point where it now makes up about 20 per cent of his practice, or about half the cases in the area. Skogstad says his focus in defending these cases is almost always the search warrant — as it was in the Holy Smoke case.

"If you succeed on the search warrant issue," he says, "you don't have to argue any of the other issues."

His success in punching holes in search warrants comes from two main factors: the Charter of Rights of Freedoms and shoddy police work. The Charter, he says, is extremely effective in protecting a private dwelling.

"It may be that a private home in Canada is the most protected place in the world. It's much easier to get a warrant in the United States, for example," he says.

His other tactic is challenging the work of police.

"It seems like they're under pressure. They seem to proceed when they don't have grounds to proceed. That means they're vulnerable in court," Skogstad says.

As proof, Skogstad points to the nine marijuana cases he handled in 1999. He won all nine. Six went to trial and were dismissed by a judge and three more were dropped by the Crown when Skogstad asked for explanations about facts relating to the warrant.

"In one of those cases I suspected trespass search. So I shot a bunch of aerial photos and I could tell that for the police to see what they said they saw, they'd have to be on the property. So I wrote to the Crown and said, 'Explain this to me.' A few weeks later the charges were dropped," he says.

Skogstad says that moment of reckoning sometimes comes in the courtroom.

"I was doing a case and the evidence suddenly changed while an officer was on the stand. It became totally inconsistent with what we had heard. It was clear there was lying going on, that's what the judge said. I'm happy to expose that," he says.

"Many times I think they say, 'I hope they plead guilty. I hope they don't get a lawyer who knows this stuff.' They try and blow it through court. I think that's a strategy."

For Skogstad, it's this abuse of civil rights that concerns him the most. One of the few groups he's joined in his life is the civil liberties subsection of the Canadian Bar Association.

"The Charter does a good job in protecting our rights but the government does not," he says.

At the same time, he understands the police frustration in fighting a war they can't win and getting little support. Skogstad says in the couple hundred marijuana-related cases he's handled while in Nelson — grow ops, possession, trafficking — he's never had a client go to jail — ever.

"Sometimes the fine is several thousand dollars, but never jail time," he says.

He worries that will change as pressure from the United States increases.

"The Americans supply surveillance data to Canadian police — they've admitted as such. Maybe it's heat signatures, maybe it shows vegetation patterns. Regardless, they're trying to convince the Canadian government they have this big problem," he says.

Despite his success, Skogstad thinks about giving up law one of these days. He wants to write books, or maybe get involved in politics. He's looking for another intellectual challenge that will replace the waning courtroom zest. At the same time, he still enjoys the brainwork.

"I like the puzzle that is each case. Especially when I figure it out."

10
Tuesday, November 17, 1997:
Murder, Mayhem, Marijuana

Ken Hammond awoke at 6 a.m. on Tuesday November 17, 1997, to a rather strange sight: a helmeted, goggled RCMP tactical officer with a very large, black gun. The officer and several others roughly got Hammond dressed and cuffed him.

"Ken Hammond, you are under arrest for the desecration of a human body," said one of the officers. They led him from his Slocan Valley trailer into the waiting squad car and drove him to the cells at the RCMP headquarters in Nelson.

Once in cells, Ken Hammond got a little bored. It was still early, around 9 a.m. So he did a very strange thing: he called the local newspaper.

The *Nelson Daily News* (my paper, remember) is a small, five-day-a-week newspaper with a circulation of roughly 5,000.

It has only five editorial employees and at 9 a.m. only one was sitting as his desk, Bruce Fuhr, the 40-something, 15-year veteran of the sports section. Fuhr had covered a lot of Junior B hockey and high school girls' volleyball games, but had never really encountered anything like Ken Hammond, an incoherent potential murderer claiming he was in jail and under investigation for, as he put it, "moving a body." Hammond even told Bruce who the alleged victim was, a 20-something named Shaun Britton.

"They're thinking about murder one," Hammond said, before hanging up.

When the phone rang the following morning, Bruce was ready with a tape recorder. They dispensed with the formalities — hey how's the jail chow, not too bad, how's the Nelson Leafs shapin' up for next season, oh pretty good. Say Ken…

Bruce: take me back through yesterday. What happened?
Hammond: well, I came out of my house yesterday morning.
Bruce: About what time?
Hammond: About six a.m., and a SWAT team came and got me.
Bruce: What do you mean, SWAT team?
Hammond: I mean guns, face coloring and camo gear and that kind of stuff.
Bruce: then what?
Hammond: They arrested me and took me to Nelson.
Bruce: Tell me the reason why they would be doing something like this?
Hammond: Zak Ackerman and Catherine Hammond, my wife. I found out they were having a fling and I went off the wall. And that's where it started, from there.
Bruce: But why would the police be implicating you in this?
Hammond: Because they implicated me in this.

Bruce: And what grounds would they have to implicate you in this?

Hammond: What do you mean, "what grounds?" Because they know Shaun and I had a fight. Shaun broke into my house.

Bruce: So did Shaun leave after the fight?

Hammond: I can't answer that, really. I can't answer it. I'm not allowed to answer that.

Bruce: So did you beat him up very bad?

Hammond: I can't answer that either. I'm not allowed to. Sorry.

Bruce: So did he ever leave your place?

Hammond: I can't answer that I guess.

Bruce: So you can't do anything. Where did you find him in the house?

Hammond: In my living room.

Bruce: When did this fight occur?

Hammond: Whenever the harvest moon was. I'm saying that because when he entered my house and I asked him what he was doing, he said it was harvest time. Understand? I guess he assumed I was growing in my house. I have no power in my house, there's no way I'm growing, you know?

Bruce: So then he broke in and you had a scuffle.

Hammond: He hit me with a CD player he had in his hands, he hit me in my eye and it just went further from there, and I can't say any more.

Bruce: But he left the place or he didn't leave the place?

Hammond: I can't answer that.

Bruce: And then it was the harvest moon, so he had been missing for about six weeks. Am I correct on this?

Hammond: Yes.

Bruce: And is that around the time you had the scuffle?

Hammond: Yes.

Bruce: So you went on with life as normal after that?

95

Hammond: No, I have not been normal ever since. My life has been off the wall. I came to the point where I wanted to kill myself. That's all I got to say, I guess.

❊　❊　❊

The following Monday, Ken Hammond was officially charged with second degree murder, to go with his human desecration charge. The coroner released the details of the autopsy: it confirmed the decomposing body found by police was indeed Shaun Britton and that he had died from a gunshot wound to the head.

Tuesday, Hammond was in court on a bail hearing, which was promptly denied. But it presented the first look at what Hammond's defense was going to be. "I think you can count on it that self-defense will be an integral component," his lawyer Blair Suffredine said.

We also got our first good look at Ken Hammond. He was a relatively short guy, maybe 5' 7", with long greasy hair pulled back in a pony tail. He had a mustache and a crazy look in his eye. As the sheriffs led him from the courthouse, Hammond began yelling at the reporters (all three of them) gathered outside that he was being set up, that they "wanted to nail him."

The RCMP also flexed their muscles about a month later, getting a search warrant to seize the *Nelson Daily News'* Hammond tapes and notes.

The long wait began. With 17 investigators and dozens of witnesses, plus a slew of forensic evidence, it would months before Ken Hammond would go to trial.

❊　❊　❊

Ken Hammond went on trial for the second degree murder of Shaun Britton at the end of October 1998, some 11 months after police found Britton's half-buried body about a mile from

Hammond's house. It was the first murder trial in Nelson in almost four years. The last one was in 1995 when Joseph Dejong beat Fred Ridden to death because he thought Ridden was threatening him with a gun which turned out to be a starter's pistol. Dejong was convicted of second degree murder, which was bumped down to manslaughter on appeal. Dejong's lawyer: Suffredine, who was now Ken Hammond's attorney.

It was obvious Suffredine was going to need all of his magic tricks to get Hammond off the hook. The story is a long and twisted tale that revealed itself over several days of testimony.

It goes like this …

Shaun Britton recently purchased a parcel of land at the base of the Slocan Valley and now he's got money problems. He's trying to sell off as much of his stuff as he can: he's offered his car and trucks to tenants and neighbors, he's hocked other stuff of value. He tells a tenant on his property he's struck a deal with someone in the Valley to trade his vehicles for marijuana. Britton's thinking it will be much quicker and easier to turn dope into cash than to take the time to sell the vehicles. He goes to meet Ken Hammond.

97

But Hammond, a former grower, hasn't got any dope. Hammond had messed around with his electricity meter in an attempt to limit the readings. That's because growing pot indoors under halide lights sucks up an incredible amount of juice, so much so that the police and the Crown often use power bills as evidence or to get warrants. Anyway, B.C. Hydro caught Hammond screwing with his meter and cut his power. No power, no pot.

But Britton doesn't know this. Hammond has a reputation in the relatively small Valley community as a grower, and Britton has no reason not to believe that trading cars for dope won't be an easy, safe deal.

Only the Lord knows what happened when Britton got to Hammond's house. Hammond says he found Britton robbing the place, they fought and Britton went through a plate glass window onto the porch and died. This is unlikely. More plausibly, Britton arrived at Hammond's and got into an argument when he realized Hammond had no dope. Argument heats up and Britton gets shot. Or Ken Hammond simply shot Shaun Britton as he walked through the door, knowing he had no dope to trade. Or he shot Shaun Britton because he's crazy. Whatever.

But forensic pathologist Dr. Laurel Gray testified at trial and she made it clear that Britton didn't die in no scrap. She testified Britton died almost instantly of two gunshot wounds from a .22 caliber gun. One bullet hit Britton in the face, just below the right cheekbone. It went through his face, shattered his left jaw, tore apart his jugular vein and carotid arteries before stopping just below his left ear. This would have been enough to kill him. Another bullet entered Britton's melon above the right eyebrow, went through his brain and then severed the medulla, the lower part of the brain that connects it with the spine. The bullet then stopped just inside the skull. This too would have been enough to kill him. Dr. Gray said she couldn't tell which bullet was fired first, but that they were both fired while Britton was still alive, indicating that they were less than a minute apart.

The autopsy had a few other interesting facts about Shaun Britton. He was half in the bag when he was shot, blood alcohol level at 0.048 (0.08 is impaired). He'd also smoked up three to four hours before getting his head invaded and had enough marijuana residue to indicate he was a habitual, heavy dope user.

Here's my theory: the bullet that goes through his face is likely the first bullet because it's fired on an angle, as Britton's head was slightly turned — like you might do if you were about get shot at. That bullet knocks him off his feet, knocks him through the plate glass window onto the porch and most likely renders him unconscious. He's going, but he's not gone yet. So the second bullet, fired from almost directly above him, finishes the job. Yow.

OK, now Hammond's got a dead guy on the porch. Well, not much I can do for him now, figures Hammond, might as well finish the transaction. His 13-year-old stepson comes home and they and a family friend drive over to Britton's place to collect the rest of his vehicles and take whatever else of value they can find, including a couple bags full of bud. The 13-year-old takes some for himself and gives the rest to step-Daddy dearest, who says he's going to sell it. Hammond sells the family friend one of Britton's trucks, who says he figured everything was on the up and up because Hammond had the ownership papers. Hammond transfers Britton's other two vehicles into his own name. Kill a guy, go to his house, steal his stuff, transfer his cars into your name and bury the body. Nobody said criminals had to be smart.

Two stepsons are back at the house the next day, helping clean up the pool of blood on the front porch. They do this grisly task in exchange for a bag of bud. Hammond tells them he caught Britton breaking into the house and had to shoot him in self-defense. The body is nowhere to be found, but there are pieces of his skull and brain around, "little pieces of Jell-O" is how one kid describes it.

Catherine Hammond comes home from a trip to Alberta a couple days later to find her husband still wearing the blood-stained clothes he shot a guy in a day before. He tosses her the keys to Shaun Britton's Buick Skylark and says, "Happy Birthday." But Catherine Hammond is one to look a gift horse in the mouth: she asks a few carefully worded questions and discovers the truth.

"Are you sure he's dead?"

"Well..." hubby answers.

So they head up the logging road where Hammond has dumped the body. He's dead alright. "First thing I saw was white socks on Shaun," Catherine testified.

Kenster wants to take the body farther up the logging road and bury Britton in the forest. He ties Britton to the back of the dead guy's Skylark. Catherine Hammond isn't faring so well. "The rope kept breaking. I was really scared," she told the court.

They drag Britton the best they can up the logging road. Catherine Hammond says she just curled up on the passenger seat and cried. Ken Hammond eventually gets out and drags the body into the woods. He returns a little while later and they head back home.

But Catherine's got the yips. She wants to call the police and tell them what happened. Ken doesn't think that's such a good idea. You'll go down too, he reminds her, not to mention your janitorially minded sons. Catherine mulls this over. She decides that getting the fuck out of there is the best course of action. She packs up her stuff and heads to Zak Ackerman's, whom she happens to be having an affair with. It's where her kids are staying as well. The affair started, she said, when her husband asked her to ask Ackerman, a mutual friend of theirs, to have a threesome with them. Ackerman said no, but he and Catherine got it on anyway.

She tells Ackerman the whole sordid tale and he convinces her to go to the police. Hammond wakes up the next morning staring into the business end of an RCMP SWAT team.

Suffredine, the defense lawyer, had few cards to play. He acknowledged before the Crown had finished its case that Hammond had indeed killed Britton. His defense was simply that he killed Britton in self-defense. But Suffredine had a problem: the evidence didn't really bear that out. Britton's shoes were missing and his coat was off, indicating he'd come in, kicked off his hush puppies, taken off his jacket and looked to stay awhile. Though Hammond told the self-defense tale to several people it was different each time.

"I punched and fought with Britton — no, wait, I hit him with a CD player, no he fell through the plate glass window and I have no idea how he ended up with two .22 caliber shells in his head."

The gun, by the way, belonged to one of Hammond's stepsons, as did the shells matching the ones in Britton's noggin.

The only one able to confirm the self-defense tale was Hammond himself, and he wasn't reliable or stable enough to put on the stand. Who knows what the crazy bastard might say. No, thought Suffredine, better just to give the jury something to think about and leave it at that. So Suffredine got up and laid the self-defense theory out without calling a single witness to back it up. In fact, Suffredine called no witnesses on Hammond's behalf at all. No friends, relatives, doctors, priests, not even the family dog came forward in defense of Ken Hammond.

Justice Mark McEwan sealed Hammond's fate when he told the jury that they couldn't consider the self-defense theory of the crime because they hadn't heard any admissible evidence to support it. It took them less than a day to convict him. On November 16, 1998, a year, a month and three days after killing Shaun Britton, Ken Hammond was convicted of his murder.

Hammond, true to form, called the *Daily News* a couple of weeks later to chat about his conviction. He said he was "in shock" and continued to proclaim his innocence. He told the reporter it was a set-up. He said he had wanted to take the stand and that his lawyer wouldn't let him.

At January's pre-sentence hearing, a doctor labelled Hammond a psychopath who was likely to re-offend. Suffredine pointed out that Hammond scored 31 on the psychopath test chart and that 30 was the minimum standard.

"Just barely a psychopath then," quipped the judge.

It was also revealed that Hammond, an American citizen, had a previous manslaughter conviction in California and the details were eerily similar: small-caliber gunshot wound to the head, Hammond stealing marijuana and vehicles from the deceased, a claim of self-defense. Hammond had in fact spent 10 of his last 13 years in jail in the U.S. and the two years he'd been in B.C. were the longest he'd been free since childhood.

So McEwan threw him in the can for good. Hammond got a life sentence with no eligibility for parole for 20 years, twice the minimum amount. He'll be almost 60 when he gets out.

11
Trial and Error

*T*he Holy Smoke trial got rolling in September and the Nelson courthouse was a gong show. There were several cops, along with the Crown attorney and his assistant, as well as the lab technician they'd flown in from Vancouver. The defendants were there with lawyers and a substantial hippie support contingent. In the small courthouse with its minimum of seating space, it made for some tight quarters and hard glances.

When the case started it looked for all the world like a simple possession and trafficking offense, something that could be wrapped up in a single day. But it became immediately apparent this case was going to be anything but simple.

The initial trouble stemmed from how the case was going to be tried. Because Skogstad wanted to question the validity of the search, this called for a separate hearing called a *voir dire*, or a trial within a trial. But Crown Rob Brown was ready to try his case. He had all the cops and witnesses waiting in the hall. He had flown in a narcotics analyst from Vancouver whose job it was to testify that the dope was indeed, beyond a scientific doubt, dope. Skogstad wanted to examine the analyst as well, but needed time to prepare. Apparently the samples had to be tested twice because the first analyst had died of a cocaine and heroin overdose. Complicating matters further, Middlemiss had decided to defend himself — which is perfectly his right under the law — but it slowed things down even more.

The legal wrangling took a day to figure out. A compromise was reached: Brown would present his case during the *voir dire*, with the understanding the evidence would be admissible at the trial itself. The reasoning was simple: if Brown lost the *voir dire* and his evidence was thrown out, there wouldn't be a case to try anyway. The case was held over until November.

The two days of testimony on November 5 and 6 were the seminal moments in the Holy Smoke case, where it was won and lost.

Det. Ernie Miller was first. Brown establishes Miller's credibility, his experience as an officer with the Vancouver City Police and with the Nelson City Police. Miller testifies that he's been involved in well over 100 drug cases.

Brown then asks Miller what he knew about Holy Smoke in the months leading up to the arrest. Brown is trying to get into evidence Miller's understanding that the Holy Smokers were pro-marijuana advocates. There is some kerfuffle about this, as Skogstad objects to the exercise of free speech being used against them in court. But Judge Takahashi gets the point: these people liked marijuana.

Brown also focuses on the proximity of the store to area schools, again emphasizizing the children in peril. Miller testifies that, yes indeedy, there are schools in the area. This is a little bogus in that Nelson is a small town and there isn't anywhere you could go and not be within walking distance of a school. (Hell, the whole *town* is within walking distance.) But the message is clear here as well: the kids are at risk.

Miller goes through the days leading up to the bust, the businessman who tells he and Scalia that marijuana is being smoked in the Holy Smoke shop, the information he has obtained from other unnamed sources that kids are smoking dope in the store. He goes through the surveillance on the day of the bust and the two guys he saw emerge (remember Charlie and Dwayne) whom Scalia got additional information from that marijuana was being smoked in the store that day. Miller testifies:

"I was informed by Scalia that individuals as young as 15 had been smoking in the Holy Smoke Culture Shop in the presence of the owners. I relayed to him the fact that I had seen six youths enter the store and that if this type of act was going on we should put a stop to it."

105

Miller testifies that he and Scalia entered the store and were immediately aware of "the obvious odor of marijuana." He searched the store, looking for the six kids he'd seen enter earlier but they were not there. He came back to the front of the store and saw a baggie of marijuana on the island behind the counter. They arrested Cantwell and then Middlemiss and Scalia took them to the station to get the warrant.

While he was waiting for Scalia to return, Miller testified, he stood outside the shop. He tells the court he went inside to use the phone once because he lost radio contact with Scalia. Scalia returned and they executed the search.

Brown then takes Miller through the pictures, 34 in all, which Miller took while executing the warrant. They then go through each exhibit, a virtual crash course on the what's what of marijuana growing and smoking. They go through all he dope Miller found — on the island, in baggies under the counter, on the desk in the back office. With that, he's done.

Cantwell's lawyer, Kenyon McGee, cross-examines Miller first. It's largely uneventful, other than one exchange where McGee asks Miller if he's ever seen *Alice in Wonderland*. He points out that the pipes Miller found in Holy Smoke were similar to the ones featured in the movie *Alice in Wonderland* — as tobacco pipes. It's all very strange.

Skogstad's cross of Miller is far more entertaining. The experienced trial lawyer, Skogstad uses a quick, curt style of questioning. He asks his questions quickly, one on top of another, trying to keep Miller off his game. This is in stark contrast to Crown attorney Brown who asks questions like he's getting paid by the hour — which he is.

Skogstad starts by emphasizing the importance of the marijuana found on the island.

SKOGSTAD: Without the marijuana on the island, you don't have anything, is that right?

MILLER: No, we could tell by the smell that marijuana was being smoked on the premises.

SKOGSTAD: But you already knew marijuana was being smoked in there, your informant told you that. It shouldn't have come as a surprise.

He quizzes Miller about using the phone while Scalia was away getting the search warrant. He wonders why he needed to use the phone if they had radios. He asks if he had permission from the owners to use the phone, whether he went into an employee area to use the phone. Skogstad is trying to get Miller to acknowledge that he was in an employee area without a warrant. He's only moderately successful here, as Miller stands his ground.

SKOGSTAD: Wants to know about the dope Miller found on the table, the basis of the warrant.

SKOGSTAD: How far away was it when you first saw it?

MILLER: Six feet.

SKOGSTAD: OK. Can you show us a photograph of where that exhibit was lying, just so we can see it better?

MILLER: No, I don't have a photograph, I'm sorry.

SKOGSTAD: you don't have a photo of it?

MILLER: No.

SKOGSTAD: What, is there one somewhere else?

Miller is shuffling his feet now, starting to look a little uncomfortable standing in the witness box.

MILLER: No I didn't take a photograph of that.

SKOGSTAD: You didn't take a photograph of this?

MILLER: — Of the island [where he found the dope] that's correct.

SKOGSTAD: You have a photos of four different shots of the back counter, none of which show marijuana. You took four shots of what is not marijuana, is that right?

MILLER: That's correct.

Skogstad: you took no shots of what was marijuana?

MILLER: I didn't have the camera then.

107

Miller's story is that the evidence bag Scalia brought him didn't have the camera in it, but he started tagging and bagging evidence without it. He started with the baggie on the island, the most important exhibit. As Skogstad goes through the photos and the corresponding exhibits with Miller, however, it becomes apparent that he cataloged and tagged several exhibits and then put them back to photograph them after the camera arrived.

SKOGSTAD: why didn't you do that with the exhibit on the island?

MILLER: I really didn't think it would be a problem. It was in plain view. It would have been a good thing to do.

SKOGSTAD: Well, Mr. Cantwell tells me and will testify at this voir dire that there was no marijuana on the island. What do you say to that?

MILLER: I would say that Mr. Cantwell is mistaken, very mistaken.

12

Ernie Miller

Ernie Miller can remember grade 11 high school career day in Port Alberni, B.C., in 1971. An RCMP officer came to talk to his class and left an indelible impression on him. When he graduated in 1973, however, married folks were forbidden to apply to the RCMP and not only had Miller gotten hitched to his high school sweetheart, he had a child on the way as well.

Fortunately for Miller, they changed the rules in 1974, so he applied right away. Unfortunately, he didn't make it. So he worked in the family sporting goods business, but being a police officer was always in the back of his mind. Though he worked eight more years at the store it was pretty obvious he didn't want to do that for the rest of his life, so he applied to the RCMP again. According to Miller it was just at the time when the crunch came for the so-called "preferred candidates" – minorities, women — certainly not stocky white guys. So he was put on hold. In the interim he applied to the Vancouver City Police Department — by this time he was 30 years old — and he was selected right away. He left Port Alberni and never looked back.

He started in the Southeast portion of Vancouver where he spent four years before being transferred to the skids on the East side where he walked a beat and dealt with the epidemic.

"The skids would have these 16-17-year-old girls and even younger, working the streets so they could get enough money so they could buy some cocaine. They'd purchase it right away and run into some alley or up some fire escape and shoot up. It was pathetic. Every day you could find drugs like that. We'd set up surveillance in Pigeon Park and watch the dealers sell dime baggies of dope. We'd go down and arrest them, it would be nothing to get five or six arrests in a day. It was so obvious, it was painful."

Miller is by nature a sensitive man. He tried valiantly to hang on to his compassion for both criminals and those ravaged by drug use, something that most cops become immune to after seeing it day after day after day. Although Miller managed to retain his humanity, he did nevertheless developed a strong hatred towards the substances abused — heroin, coke … and marijuana.

"I can remember talking to this girl, this hooker I caught shooting up in Vancouver, and you looked at her and she was just a pathetic sight. She was full of sores, very sickly looking but she had the prettiest eyes, beautiful blue. She was probably at one time a very pretty girl. She told me that she started with marijuana and when she wasn't getting a high out of it anymore, when she got used to it, she tried other drugs. It was a long, slippery slope from there. Whether marijuana was to blame, it's hard for me to say. That's what she said."

After three years on the streets, Miller became a member of the elite Emergency Response Team. It was very busy, work-wise and court-wise, and it kept Miller away from home for long stretches. It wasn't conducive to a good family life, something that was important to him. It was different from the skids, but in some ways even more stressful. By 1990 Miller was already thinking about ways to get away from big city policing when events conspired to convince him it was time to go.

"It was an emergency response call for 911 from a Vietnamese or Asian family. There was a language barrier, but apparently there was a shooting at this house. We were directed to an upstairs bedroom and I was the first one in there. Mother and father were shot in the head. An eight-year-old girl shot in the head. A baby shot in the stomach, dead. And the guy, the suspect, turned the gun on himself. It bothered me substantially because I identified with these children. With my own children. You tend to do that in these situations, or I do anyway. I had children around the same age. So I gave it some thought afterwards and that was just about enough. I didn't want to be in there anymore."

111

Early in 1991 Miller's father passed away and it changed his perspective even further. He realized that if he didn't strengthen the relationship with his family he ran the risk of losing them.

"If you don't have family when you retire in this job, you don't have anything. It made me realize how short life really is. June 1st, 1992, I was sworn in in Nelson. The move has been good for our family, the kids are still here, we have a couple of grandkids now, so things have worked out well."

For Miller, Nelson offered the kind of hands-on police work that he enjoyed most and that he was most skilled at — it was a model for community policing.

"No call too small, police always available, if you have a problem let's work at it together. It's more proactive here," he says. It was easier on the family and easier on his psyche.

"Regular patrol, regular shifts. It took some getting used to after seven-and-a-half years in Vancouver. They have an alert tone when something important — man with a gun, or robbery in progress — is happening. It took me some time to get used to not hearing that. It was kind of nice," Miller says.

What was also nice was the relative lack of drugs on the streets of Nelson.

"There are drugs here. But the most prominent drug on the street here is marijuana. There is some other stuff, cocaine mostly, but no great amounts," he says.

He worries, first and foremost, about the kids, of which he now has three, two in their twenties and one in her teens.

"My youngest daughter, she's quite outspoken about it, she doesn't agree with marijuana. At least that's what she tells me," he says.

It was Miller's youngest daughter who further substantiated his suspicion that the owners of Holy Smoke were peddling weed to minors.

"Well, she was hearing that they were selling to kids. When we busted them, some kids came to her and said they were upset because they didn't have anywhere to go to buy their dope."

For Miller, that was simply not acceptable. He'd come too far and seen too many good kids suffer to let it happen here too.

Sgt. Franklin Antonio Scalia is first on the stand for the prosecution the next day. He too goes through his qualifications — eight years with the NCP, nine years before that with the Vancouver Police Department, including undercover drug operations in some of Van's seediest locales. He testifies that he's been involved in drug cases numbering "in the high hundreds."

Scalia recounts his conversations with businesspeople in the neighborhood in the days before the bust. He talks about their concerns that the owners of Holy Smoke were selling to kids. He acknowledges he looked up the criminal records of the accused.

On the day of the bust, Scalia testifies that when Miller notified him of the two kids they knew coming from Holy Smoke, he followed them down to Baker Street and confronted them. He says he smelled cannabis on their breath and on their clothes. He arrested them and took them into the foyer of the Medical Arts building on Baker Street. There he searched them, found a small amount of dope on one of the suspects and began his questioning. He found out that they had been smoking marijuana in the store. He took the one he found the dope on down to the station and went to get Miller.

"We decided the best and only course of action was to put a stop to it. I didn't feel we had grounds for a warrant, but we had to put a stop to the activity."

Scalia describes the initial search, about Miller pointing out the baggie of bud on the island. He arrested Middlemiss and Cantwell and took them to the station, but released them pending the search. Scalia then tells the court that he got a written statement from the kid he's arrested on Baker Street and that he went to get the warrant. He acknowledges that he was in a hurry, worried about his partner guarding the shop with potential hostile folks milling around. With warrant in hand, he returned to the store, in the process forgetting the camera.

Brown then takes Scalia through the exhibits, much as he had Miller. Scalia is much smoother than Miller, much more polished. His vocabulary is larger and he is well-spoken — especially for a cop. He is always much more confident, much quicker on his feet.

Skogstad is ready. He starts with the informant Scalia arrested on Baker Street who'd told him he'd just smoked up in Holy Smoke.

Skogstad: I understand that you said when you released [the informant Pullen] you told him he was subject to a summons [for possession].

Scalia: Correct.

Skogstad: But no summons was ever issued.

Scalia: No.

Skogstad: And you told him that he wouldn't have to go to court if he helped you.

Scalia: No, I didn't tell him that.

Skogstad: Then why didn't you summons him?

Scalia: I had no reason to, really.

Skogstad: Then why did he help you?

Scalia: He cooperated with me. I know this individual. He has been cooperative in the past. He was cooperative that day.

Skogstad gets Scalia to acknowledge that the guy told him he smoked his own marijuana and that he didn't buy it at the store, and that the owners discouraged people from smoking in the store.

114

Though it wasn't necessarily apparent at the time, Skogstad was picking off the points of the warrant one by one. He had shredded Miller on the baggie of marijuana on the island, and Miller's failure to photograph it while photographing everything else under the sun. He had questioned Scalia's informant source, at least raising the possibility that the guy would have told Scalia anything to save his own skin from a possession charge and that he had been successful because Scalia didn't charge him.

Now Skogstad is after the businessmen who saw drug transactions in front of the shop, another basis for the warrant. He wants to know exactly what these businessmen have seen. Scalia replies that they saw people passing things back and forth in the alley during lunch hour and after school. Could it have been leaflets? Cigarettes? Pokemon cards? Scalia says they couldn't exactly say but points to the Holy Smoke owners' criminal records — a cultivation charge against DeFelice and trafficking charge against Middlemiss. They're drug dealers.

But what about the businessmen who saw drug deals. Have they ever been in the store? No. And then Skogstad raises a very interesting point: why would the owners of Holy Smoke sell drugs in the alley outside their store in full view of the world when they could do it in their basement store where nobody could see in? Scalia doesn't have an answer for that. In the end Scalia acknowledges that the transactions witnessed by the businessman were "possible" drug transactions, not "probable" drug transactions.

And that was it for the Crown. Remember, it's a *voir dire*, not the actual trial. All Brown has to establish is that the warrant was legally obtained and then the trial would begin. After two days, though, they were out of time, and the case was held over again, until January 1999.

That was also the month that Holy Smoke reached a deal on their business license for 1998. There had been much wrangling and negotiation between representatives for the city and representatives for Holy Smoke and representatives for other businesses, principally Suffredine. Some of the more liberal members of council had already brought the issue back to the council, specifically proposing that Holy Smoke's business license be brought back in line with the rest of the businesses.

Municipal elections in Nelson were to be held in 1999. The campaigning was already beginning in January and several current councillors were rumored to have aspirations to the mayor's chair — and Mayor Exner hadn't ruled out another term, though it was being suggested that he might run for the Liberals provincially. Regardless, nobody wanted another long, nasty court battle with several prominent businesses, and nobody wanted to look like the big, bad wolf picking on Holy Smoke — at least not in an election year.

So the city backed down. Though they refused to release details of the settlement, the Holy Smokers say they paid their $120 and nothing more. The city agreed to change business license fee structure — no more $1000 bills for bong pipe sellers. Holy Smoke had won that battle. One down, one to go.

Skogstad's witnesses in the *voir dire* were minimal. He called Cantwell, who testified that not only was there no marijuana on the island, the marijuana the police allegedly found was crappy, shitty marijuana.

"We wouldn't have anything like that in this store."

Dangerously, Cantwell admitted that they had marijuana in the store, that each of the owners had their own private stash. But he maintained there was none on the island, in the open, on that day.

116

Skogstad also brought forward a witness who said she called the store on the day of the bust and that somebody answered "Nelson City Police." When she inquired as to where Cantwell and the other owners were, she was told they were on their way to jail. It was important testimony because it indicated that Miller hadn't just used the phone to call Scalia, but that he might have answered it while waiting for Scalia inside the store.

There was not much else. By the time Skogstad was done, the various delays had dragged a one-day possession charge case into a several-month ordeal. Justice Takahashi reserved ruling, saying he would hand it down in written form. There was nothing to do but wait.

13

The Decision

*J*ustice Takahashi's ruling dropped like a bomb. Skogstad phoned the *Daily News* to let me know it had been released. He left a message on my voice mail: "You are not going to believe this."

Takahashi threw all the evidence out, claiming it was the result of a bad search. He vilified the police. It was an absolute shit-kicking.

In his written ruling he first dealt with Det. Miller.

"Miller took pictures of the interior of the Shop but no pictures of the drugs inside the Shop. He gave no satisfactory explanation for this omission."

Takahashi also questioned versions of events regarding the use of the telephone.

"How was it that Miller could be in the Shop to answer the phone at least 30 minutes before he talked with Scalia? This was not explained."

Takahashi went even further.

"Miller discovered the drugs. The determination that Miller is a reliable witness is a precondition to finding that the drugs were found 'in plain sight.' I cannot make this determination. In all circumstances I find the evidence of the defense more compelling. I find that the discovery of the drugs came from an illegal search."

Takahashi was basically saying he believed a pot smoker and his buddies over the word of a police officer. It was, to say the least, astonishing.

But Takahashi wasn't done. He picked apart the warrant, count by count:

1. The source felt that the proprietors were selling drugs, as there were transactions seen and a high volume of traffic to and from the store.

118

"The 'feeling' that drugs were being sold was based on fact. The use of 'proprietors' was wrong since Scalia could not recall if the source said he saw more than one Defendant and no Defendant was specifically identified. This paragraph did not assist to determine whether a crime was being committed or that evidence would likely be found in the Shop.

2. The Holy Smoke Culture Shop is a store devoted to the sale of drug paraphernalia, specifically cannabis products, and the promotion of marijuana and its derivatives.

"Scalia denied that this paragraph was drafted to falsely suggest that cannabis products were sold at the Shop but the awkward punctuation could allow for that interpretation. Information that the Shop sold paraphernalia used in consumption of cannabis and materials promoting the legalization of marijuana is not probative of the issues.

3. The proprietors of the Holy Smoke Culture Shop openly advocate the repeal of Canadian drug laws pertaining to cannabis.

"This paragraph is not probative of the issues."

4. Subsequent to the initial information obtained, on October 15, 1997, Sgt. Scalia received information that more than one person was smoking marijuana in the Holy Smoke Culture Shop with consent of the owner.

"Scalia only had information that the youth informant smoked in the Shop that day. The statement that 'more than one person' smoked marijuana in the Shop was a misrepresentation. The use of the present tense and the omission of the information that the youth informant used his own marijuana made this paragraph capable of being misunderstood to mean that there were drugs and ongoing criminal activity in the shop."

5. At 1215 hours, October 15, 1997, Sgt. Scalia and Det. Miller attended the Holy Smoke Culture Shop... immediately upon entry both officers noted a heavy smell of marijuana smoke... Det. Miller subsequently noted a bag of marijuana (bud) lying in plain view on the counter used by employees.

"The smell was consistent with the youth informant using marijuana in the store shortly before. It did not necessarily imply the existence of marijuana on the premises. I have found that Miller did not find the bag in plain view and I delete this from consideration.

119

6. ... Middlemiss entered the store and was arrested by Det. Miller. He was searched and found to be in personal possession of a small quantity of marijuana.

"Miller arrested Middlemiss because he was an owner of the Shop and the smell of marijuana was detected in the Shop. Middlemiss entered the Shop after police. Miller did not have sufficient grounds to arrest Middlemiss. The arrest was without proper grounds which made the search illegal.

"Paragraph 7 does not add information which may be useful in determining whether a search warrant should have been granted.

"Without consideration of the Drugs in the Shop the Information lacks evidence on which to infer that drugs or criminal activity will be found in the Shop. I find that the Warrant is invalid."

Now, that could have been it right there. Takahashi said he didn't believe Miller's testimony and that Scalia deliberately misrepresented the facts to get the search warrant. He had tossed out the evidence and crushed the case. But was not finished yet. He wanted to send a message. The third section of Takahashi's decision is entitled, "Reputation and the Administration of Justice." It is a tongue-lashing of the first order:

120

"The drugs are real evidence but without further evidence the police could not legally gain access to the shop to discover it.

The arrest of Cantwell, Middlemiss and the customers was without a proper basis to believe they were in possession of a drug and demonstrates a cavalier attitude towards the laws of arrest and search.

The drafting of the information was troubled by the inclusion of mildly inflammatory non-probative facts and shading of phrases through the use of punctuation and verb tense which subtly introduced the possibility of prejudicial construction.

The police cannot claim the benefit of good faith. This was lost by the staging of the drugs, the misrepresentations in the information, the misrepresentations at trial in the disregard of the Charter.

The possession and trafficking of illegal substances is a serious concern of the public, particularly when young persons are victims. In this case the trafficking of illegal substances to young persons was hypothesized but never proven.

The search and seizure procedures have been established to balance the concerns of the citizens to:

1. arrest, prosecute, and where appropriate, to convict people who are breaking the law; and ;

2. to be free from unreasonable invasion of their privacy by the police.

The administration of justice in this case cannot endorse the behavior of the police without a loss of reputation.

I rule that the evidence adduced on the voir dire be excluded."

This wasn't a victory for the Holy Smokers — it was an ol' fashioned ass kicking. Not only did they beat the rap, but the police who had so obviously tried to target them were called liars and frauds by a provincial court judge.

Considering the magnitude of their victory the Holy Smokers were surprising humble. There was no gloating. A few comments about the importance of free speech in light of the fact that the police had tried to use their marijuana decriminalization advocacy in court, but nothing along the lines of, Nah, nah, we won and you lost. Privately, the Holy Smokers would acknowledge that while they were jubilant in their victory, rubbing the cops noses' in it hardly seemed like a smart idea.

It was actually the lawyer Skogstad who made the most stinging comments, questioning police methodology, claiming "it wasn't up to snuff."

Reaction from the other side was non-existent. The police, Crown Attorney Brown and the mayor all refused comment. It was surprising, especially in Exner's case, since he was never shy for words. But this was a stunning defeat and nobody could think of anything to say.

The hardest hit was Miller. There were rumors in the days following the ruling that he was considering resigning from the Nelson City Police. He felt humiliated and shamed. He wondered if he could ever do his job again.

Reaction in the community was predictably mixed. On one side, dope smokers and liberals celebrated a ruling that challenged the power of the police to behave as they wished. Many were happy to see the NCP — and Scalia in particular — get their comeuppance. On the other hand, much of the community supported the police. Damn hippies, they got lucky, won on a technicality. Those who believed in law and order still supported the NCP and their officers.

Two weeks after Takahashi's written ruling, all parties reconvened in court and agreed to dismiss the charges, considering the crucial evidence had been thrown out. Takahashi dismissed the charges. So on April 26, 1999, over a year after the case began and almost 20 months after the bust, Holy Smoke was finally in the clear.

14
Dope 101

123

Marijuana, cannabis, dope, bud, reefer, weed, mary jane, pot, doobie, jay, sensimilla, ganja, grass, Acapulco gold.

Botanically speaking, it is all part of the Cannabacae family of plants and a member of the genus cannabis. Generally speaking there are three species: the most common is the Cannabis sativa, a tall, gangly pot plant that grows as high a twenty feet. Big bud. Cannabis indica is shorter in height, maybe three or four feet and shaped like a pyramid. Cannabis ruderalis, which has by far the best name in my humble opinion, is smaller still and with almost no branches or stems. This is the basic scientific naming stuff that we all flunked in high school; just remember cannabis sativa and you'll be fine. There is no test later.

Contained within cannabis are more than 460 known com-pounds, of which 60-plus are known as cannabinoids and the cannabinoid that we've all come to know and love is 3,4-trans-delta-l-tetrahydrocannabinol, also known as delta-1-THC, delta-9-THC, or simply THC. This THC is good stuff, the highly pyschoactive agent that gives marijuana its punch. It's what makes the high. The THC element comes from the resin that covers the flowering part of female cannabis plants. The resin is thought to be used by the plant to protect it from heat and preserve moisture for reproduction. That's why buds are valuable, while the leaves and the stalks — or *shake* as it's known — doesn't give the same kind of buzz. The resin by itself is known as hashish, or hash and comes in sticky little pieces or in oil form. In other words, hash oil is marijuana resin — it's where the THC lives. Cannabis without THC is known as hemp.

Cannabis has a long and storied history. It first pops up in central Asia, perhaps as long as 10,000 years ago. The first recorded cultivation occurs in China by 4000 BC and it first appears in Chinese medical texts around 2000 BC. From there, cannabis is used by societies all across Asia, India, the Middle East and Africa. It is prescribed for a litany of illnesses includ-ing malaria, dysentery, headaches, insomnia. It was used to improve digestion, cure nausea, and as an anesthetic. It was the Aspirin of its time.

And that time includes thousands of years of history and almost every major society, from the Romans to Victorian-era England. It's used as a drug and, as hemp, as a fiber to make rope, sails, clothes and paper. The oil is used to make soap and fuel. Good ol' cannabis is one handy little weed.

It is also a fixture in the New World. Though we are starting to get into folklore territory here, there are those who claim that Cartier and Champlain brought hemp over with them, or discovered it soon after arriving. There is more conclusive evidence that hemp was a staple crop of early North American settlers.

The point is — and I could go on and on and on about this — cannabis has been a widely accepted source of medicine and fuel for thousands of years. It is, by far, one of the most hearty, useful substances on the planet. So what happened?

Well, crazy-ass North American politics is the short answer. The medium answer is, a combination of factors including corporate greed and racism on both sides of the border.

Things were going fairly tickety-boo for cannabis until the turn of the 20th century. Then in 1930, right around the time Henry Ford is building a car to run on hemp fuel, the U.S. gets caught up in prohibition and race hysteria. Marijuana becomes stigmatized as the drug of Asians, Mexicans and African-Americans — hardly surprising considering those cultures had embraced cannabis long before. The FBI, under a fellow by the name of Henry Anslinger, puts together an intensive propaganda campaign against marijuana. It portrays dope-smoking Mexican banditos as a menace to society. Anslinger goes before Congress and testifies that marijuana leads to violent, psychotic behavior — despite the fact that no scientifically accepted study had ever said that.

125

Not coincidentally, around this time DuPont chemicals is experimenting with and patenting the process by which plastics are made. Things like nylon are now possible — a tough durable fiber that has limitless potential and only one major competitor: hemp. Though a collusionary effort between chemical, forestry and pharmaceutical companies has never been proven, it is often alluded to by those inclined to believe in conspiracy theories. Companies in bed with government: who would have thunk it?

The result of this mess is something called the Marijuana Tax Act, passed in 1937. It stipulates that anyone using marijuana for industrial or medical uses has to pay a tax of $1 an ounce. Anyone in the possession of marijuana for any other reason was subject to a $100-an-ounce tax. Heavy fines are levied for evading the tax. The law is squarely aimed at the recreational pot user. Cannabis is removed from the United States Pharmacopoeia and National Formulary in 1941 and 4000 years of medical history are effectively wiped off the map.

One of the few public officials who responded rationally to the issue of marijuana in the 1930s was New York's Mayor Fiorello LaGuardia. In 1938 he appointed a committee of scientists to study the medical, sociological, and psychological aspects of marijuana use in New York City. Two internists, three psychiatrists, two pharmacologists, a public health expert, the commissioners of Correction, Health, and Hospitals, and the director of the Division of Psychiatry of the Department of Hospitals made up the committee. They began their investigations in 1940 and presented detailed findings in 1944 under the title "The Marijuana Problem in the City of New York." This largely disregarded study dispelled many of the myths that had spurred passage of the Tax Act. The committee found no proof that major crime was associated with marijuana or that it caused aggressive or antisocial behavior; marijuana was not sexually overstimulating and did not change personality; there was no evidence of acquired tolerance. The study was completely ignored.

The origins of Canadian drug laws took a bit of a different route. They begin with the Chinese "coolies" who were brought to Canada to construct the Western arm of the Canadian Pacific Railway. Labor unrest in Vancouver, ostensibly caused by hatred of the Chinese by white workers, brought then Deputy Minister of Labor William Lyon McKenzie King out to assess the situation. The result: "The Need for the Suppression of Opium Traffic in Canada." This report was apparently based

126

on newspaper stories depicting the ruin of white women caused by opium use.

King's report led to the creation of the Opium Narcotic Act of 1908, which prohibited the import, manufacture and sale of opiates for non-medical purposes. The Opium Narcotic Act of 1908 has provided the basis for all other Canadian legislation dealing with the use of illicit drugs to this day, despite the fact that it was created solely to eliminate what was viewed as an undesirable element from the labor pool, and gave no regard to medical, social, or any other scientific research to back up its necessity or wisdom. In fact, it is doubtful that MacKenzie King had ever intended the Act to be applied to any segment of the white population at all.

In 1922, a series of articles appeared in *Maclean's* magazine on the illicit drug trade. They were written by Mrs. Emily Murphy, Canada's first women magistrate under the pen name Janey Canuck. They were heavily influenced by Murphy's Orange Order ties and racist anti-marijuana rhetoric. In one chapter, a Los Angeles County Chief of Police was quoted as saying that "persons using this narcotic smoke the dry leaves of the plant, which has the effect of driving them completely insane. The addict loses all sense of moral responsibility. Addicts to this drug, while under its influence, are immune to pain. While in this condition they become raving maniacs and are liable to kill or indulge in any forms of violence to other persons, using the most savage methods of cruelty without, as said before, any sense of moral responsibility." The articles led to marijuana being included in the Opium Narcotic Drug Addict.

127

OK, so let's review: Good plant used for medicine and other stuff for thousands of years by hundreds of cultures, only to be wiped out in 30 years because the Americans hate Mexicans and Canadians hate the Chinese. Can this be right? Am I missing something here?

In the early 1970s, both the Canadian and American Medical Associations agreed that marijuana is not a narcotic. The Le Dain Commission was appointed in Canada to undertake a complete and factual study of marijuana use and its effects. The results of the study were presented to the government after four years and four million dollars' worth of research.

Like the New York La Guardia study of 1944, the Le Dain Commission recognized that the use of marijuana is not linked to violent crime in any way. It also concluded that prohibitionary laws have only served to create a sub-culture with little respect for the law and law enforcement, as well as diverting law enforcement capability, clogging the judicial system, and providing a base of funds for organized crime. The recommendations of the Le Dain Commission ranged from outright legalization to small fines for marijuana use.

But crazy-ass North American politics have prevailed on both sides of the border since and despite commissions like La Guardia and Le Dain. Whether or not dope smoking is less harmful to society than the waste of dollars and police manhours used to fight it is a moot question. As long as pledging to crack down gets votes, cracking down will be what happens.

Nelson Mayor Gary Exner.

Above and at left: Sofisticated grow operations in the
Nelson area.

Convicted murderer Ken Hammond is led from the Nelson courthouse. – Jim Demers photo.

All the illicit substances found by the Nelson City Police when they busted the Holy Smoke Culture Shop in Nelson B.C. on October XX, 1997.

The cigar box full of pre-packaged, weighed and labeled marijuana found by Nelson City Police under the counter at the Holy Smoke Culture Shop during their search. Police contended the marijuana was packaged for sale, Holy Smoke owners said it was for medicinal users only.

A counter inside the employee area of the Holy Smoke Culture Shop, with various items of marijuana paraphenalia.

Alan Middlemiss, Dustin 'Sunflower' Cantwell and Paul DeFelice outside the Nelson Courthouse.
– Lara Schroeder/Nelson Daily News photo

15

Cops and the Finger in the Dam

*R*CMP Constable Bill Clay is working a checkstop one evening just outside Nelson, looking for impaired drivers, when a 20-something in a Toyota Tercel 4WD Wagon pulls up.

"Had anything to drink tonight, sir?" Clay asks.

"No sir." The kid doesn't look particularly suspicious or nervous.

"Where you headed?"

"Just home."

Clay leans forward, closer to the open window of the car so he can look into the back seat and passenger side — standard procedure — when he smells the overpowering smell of fresh marijuana.

"Hey, you got any drugs in the car?"

"What?" The kid's face flashes a moment of panic.

"Pull over to the side please."

Clay does a quick search of the front seats while the kid stands nervously at the side of the road. He wants to stop what's going on, but can't. Clay finds a sealed Tupperware container under the seat with a baggie of dope inside. It's a small amount, maybe a quarter of an ounce.

"This all you have?" Clay leans out of the car and asks the kid as he holds up the baggie.

"Yes sir."

Clay ponders this for a moment. Twenty-two years with the RCMP, eighteen with drug enforcement, currently the drug awareness officer at the Nelson detachment, Clay is the cop that testifies at trial as the dope expert. His instincts and his experience tell him that this can't be all there is. He goes around the driver's side and uses the trunk release to pop the hatchback. He finds a spare tire, a bottle of windshield washer fluid, some cardboard boxes, a few tools and a large, hiking knapsack. The smell of marijuana is stronger than ever.

Clay opens the knapsack and finds a garbage bag. Inside the garbage are several more Tupperware containers. Inside the Tupperware containers are six half-pound bags of marijuana.

"Uh oh," says Clay. He goes over to the kid to show him what he's found. The young man is distraught and Clay does his best to keep him calm. He explains what's going to happen: that he will be arrested and charged, his car towed but he should be home in his own bed tonight.

"Hell, you'll be home before I will." His tone is entirely pleasant and friendly and the kid even manages a small smile. When the time comes, Clay cuffs with his hands in front where it is far more comfortable than in the back. As he sticks him in the cruiser, the kid asks Clay: "How'd you know, man?"

"My friend, marijuana stinks. Even sealed up tight, the smell gets on the bag, in your clothes, on your hands. You stink like weed."

The kid nods.

A little later, Clay will shake his head at the memory. You know what the funny thing is: that kid, if it's his first offense will get probation, maybe a fine. Certainly no jail time. He won't get anything, really.

Life wasn't always this easy for Const. Clay. Doing hundreds upon hundreds of drug investigations in the Lower Mainland — including undercover ops in some of Vancouver's seediest neighborhoods — Clay has seen a lot of dirty water pass under the bridge. He talks almost fondly of the time when heroin dealers on Granville Street would walk around with a balloon full of capsules in their mouths, popping it out to service buyers — and swallowing it if the cops swooped in.

"Some of those guys would even use Ex-lax to speed the recovery process along," he says. "Not too much of that going on these days, cops grabbing dealers by the throats so they won't swallow the evidence. Street dealers aren't getting busted for minimal weight anymore, better to use decks." Decks are folded up pieces of paper with the drugs inside, commonly used to distribute cocaine.

131

Clay can remember the time when the three pounds of weed he took off the kid at the checkstop would've amounted to a major bust.

"In 1979 we were moving in to bust this guy just outside of Langley. We're in the full SWAT gear, crawling across the field in front of his house, when we hear this quacking, this really loud quacking. The guy had ducks, who are really easily riled, who quack when they hear a pop can rolling down the sidewalk three blocks away, as guards. So the ducks are going absolutely crazy because there's a whole team of RCMP SWAT in the yard. The guy comes out on the porch of the house with a shotgun and starts blasting away into the field. I don't think he could see us, but he knew something no good was out there — the guard ducks were telling him. He didn't hit anybody but it was scary as shit.

"Anyway, he went back inside and we got to the door, knocked it down and took him without too much problem. He had three pounds of dope and it seemed like the biggest bust in the world."

Const. Clay is not your average cop — though he looks like one. At 5' 8" and fighting the onslaught of middle age pounds, having already lost the war against the receding hairline, Clay has a reputation among cops and druggies of being fair-minded, intelligent and thoughtful. Frank Scalia likes him, and so does Dustin Cantwell.

"I think that reputation comes from telling it like it is, whether that's on the stand on in the street," says Clay, who testifies in maybe a dozen drug-related trials a year as an expert.

"If it's a home-grown operation that's obviously for personal use, then that's what I'll say. If it's churning out several pounds every three months with plants on a rotating basis, with tons of cash around and scales and baggies... well, what are you using those scales for, weighing tea? Give me a fucking break."

On the other hand, says Clay, if the operation is just a couple of plants, obviously for personal use — or personal use plus a few friends — then Clay will say that too. Clay says that more than once he has received tips from neighbors, landlords, friends or enemies that a certain house was home to a marijuana grow op[grow operation]. Checking it out, he's surmised that the operation was small-time.

"So I will go to the door, knock, and when the guy answers, I'll be straight with him: 'Look, I think you've got a grow op here, but my guess is it's pretty small. Show it to me and if it's small time, I'll leave you alone. If it isn't small time, then I'd call your lawyer.' Most guys will take you to the basement and when they show me their three dinky plants, I just tell them to get rid of it. And they're so grateful, they usually do."

Clay doesn't do this because he likes the dopers, or because he approves of their behavior. He does it out of the practicality of knowing that it isn't worth his time and effort to put these guys in the system for the minimal punishment — if any — they'll receive. And because he does subscribe to a simple philosophy: live and let live.

"Look, if somebody wants to smoke a little reefer in the privacy of their own home, and they're a mature adult perfectly capable of making their own decisions, then I say, 'Fill your boots.' It's not my choice, but if you are legitimately not hurting anybody, it's not worth my time to mess with you. If that's what you do to relax, fine. I smoke, I drink a couple of beers now and then, and I can see how people will say that's not so different. But marijuana is against the law — period. You may disagree with that, but there is a democratic way you can go about changing it. You choose to live here, you follow the system, right or wrong. My job, whether I like it or not, agree with it or not, is to enforce that law. So as soon as you take your pot use and make that someone else's problem, then I'm pretty much forced to do something. Until then, what you do is your own business."

133

Most of the guys that get caught either growing or smoking do so because they are just plain stupid or can't keep their mouths shut.

"Some of these guys get a really good crop and they're proud of themselves so they tell their buddies, who tell their buddies, and soon enough in a small town like this everybody knows —

including us," he says. "At that point, you're making us look bad, like we aren't doing our jobs. So now we have to go after you."

He has a simple message to ensure dope grower and smoking success:

"Shut the fuck up."

Clay feels that guys who flaunt their dope success are rubbing the cops' noses in it, whether intentionally or not. Police officers, always a prideful bunch, are more inclined to act when their integrity is being threatened by a bunch of long hairs. If they conduct their business in private — and keep it small time — Clay says in most cases they can operate relatively worry-free.

Clay makes it clear that he doesn't say these things because he approves — it's sheer practicality. He says if he had a hundred guys and six months, he'd love to go around the West Kootenays and bust dope growers and pot smokers until the cows came home. Even then he's not sure that it would make any significant impact on the dope trade.

He points to the RCMP Green Team, a special unit put together by the Nelson detachment to deal specifically with grow operations in the summer of 1998. The officers busted an average of two to three grow operations a week for the entire six-month period of the operation. It was deemed an unqualified success — with the acknowledgement that it had negligible impact on the dope trade in the region. It wasn't continued.

"It's a matter of resources," says Clay. "With the manpower and money we have, we need to make sure our priorities are right. Every time we take a member away from Traffic or Major Crimes, that unit suffers. We need to have cops investigating rapes and murders. We need to have cops keeping the roads safe. The thing about marijuana ops is that they will be there tomorrow if you don't get to them today."

This is a harm-reduction argument.

Like Frank Scalia, Clay believes the answer lies with education. His job as Drug Awareness Officer puts him front and center in schools trying to get the message across to kids regarding the ills of marijuana. Like most of his other dealings, Clay takes the straight-on approach.

"I don't go in there and tell kids, 'Marijuana will kill you, don't do it.' They'd laugh me out of the room. I tell them that marijuana is an unhealthy choice, like cigarettes or alcohol. I mean, you are putting smoke in your lungs, that can't be good, right?"

Clay says it amazes him that if he asks kids if they think smoking is disgusting, almost an entire class will raise their hands. But if he asks them if marijuana smoking is disgusting, only two or three will lift their arms.

"What's the difference?"

Clay says he also emphasizes that kids can't be sure what effect marijuana will have on their bodies or their lives.

"I tell them, are you going to wake up in the morning if you smoke a joint the night before? Probably. Almost definitely. But you have no idea how that joint will affect you in other ways, or even over the long term. Everybody is different. Why take any chances?"

135

Clay is a big proponent of the controversial Drug Abuse Resistance Education or D.A.R.E. program. Initially implemented in California, D.A.R.E. is targeted at grade five and six students to "equip elementary school children with skills to recognize and resist social pressures to experiment with tobacco, alcohol and other drugs," according to the promotional literature. The program is divided into 16 separate lessons, each approximately 30 to 45 minutes covering such topics as "Understanding the effects of mind altering drugs,", "Learning resistance techniques, ways to say no," and "Reducing violence."

Critics of the program have labelled it "blatant war on drugs propaganda" and "an attempt by law enforcement to brainwash our kids." Clay says those sentiments show ignorance of the program.

"This program as much as anything else teaches life skills — how to cope with the difficulties of adolescence and everyday life. It tackles self-esteem issues, stress issues, bullying issues — things that lead to drug use, among other things. How can that be bad?"

Clay has introduced the program into several schools in the communities around Nelson and is working with the Nelson City Police to try and get the program into the city's schools. He too has come up against resistance.

"I had this one lady say we were preaching our anti-drug stance to kids and that because the program was American that it wasn't right for Canadian kids — there's a lot of talk about gun and gun safety for example. Those kind of things don't happen here, she said." He shakes his head.

136

"This was just before Columbine — and then Taber and finally Ottawa. I saw her and I said: 'Think this stuff is relevant now?'" he says. "I gave all the course material for concerned parents. We ask them to look through it and usually when they read the lesson plans and go through the workbooks, they see it's not what they think."

The bottom line, according to Clay, is that a good number of these parents are having a puff or two at home and don't want their kids turned against them.

"Most dope smokers want some kind of reassurance that what they're doing is OK, that it's not bad. And when their kid comes home and says, 'Daddy, are you sure you should be smoking that?' it messes with their world."

Clay is the same as most other Kootenay cops and politicians in that he is inflexible when it comes to kids. While he's more than willing to be flexible in the cat and mouse game between cops and dope growers and pot smokers, the inclusion of kids in the mix makes his blood boil. Which is why he has very little respect for the Holy Smoke owners who violate the two Clay rules: they involve kids in the equation and they refuse to shut the fuck up.

"Look, we know that they let kids smoke up in there. They deny it, but we know it. They say they don't sell stuff to kids, like pipes and papers but we know that too. If they aren't pandering to kids then why not say, 'OK, nobody under the age of 19 is even allowed inside the fucking door. You can't come in to look around. You can't come in and be exposed to all the smoking and crazy shit that's going on down there.' Why not do that?"

Clay points out that strip clubs and even sex shops can operate in small towns like Nelson because they keep a relatively low profile and they keep kids out.

The other part of the Holy Smoke operation that frustrates Clay is the constant yapping and the hypocrisy he sees in it.

"These guys are constantly talking about how good dope is for you. Give me a break. How is it good for you? Is it good for your body? No. Is it good for your brain, does it make you smarter? No. Look at those guys and tell me how smart that is."

137

Clay thinks the Holy Smoke court case is a joke, that their tune changed as soon as they realized that they were going down.

"The day they got busted, they were crowing, 'This is a great day. We're going to go take this to the Supreme Court and get the laws on marijuana changed.' I was like, great good for you, good luck. Now when the shit actually came down, what did they do? They tried to get off on a technicality. What a crock. What a great stand to take. They know they had dope in that store. Hell, there's dope in there right now. So why not admit it and fight the fight fairly instead of trying to weasel out of it?" he says.

He points out that the marijuana they found in the store was packaged in baggies with labels indicating the weight, just as it would be if it was being made available for sale. He doesn't buy the argument recently forwarded by the Holy Smokers that the drugs were for medicinal users — and even if they were, that's no excuse.

On the issue of medical marijuana, Clay is flexible, however. Though he questions the medical validity of its use, he is reluctant to toss out the raft of anecdotal evidence that marijuana helps people who are suffering.

"If someone has cancer and they are suffering and they say that marijuana helps get them through the night, who am I to say that's not the case?" he says.

He believes however — as most other cops do — that the medicinal argument is being used as a smokescreen (pun intended) to promote widespread drug use. Holy Smoke's argument that they possess and distribute marijuana for strictly medicinal uses is laughable. To Clay, a man who treats ganja growers with respect, this violates his sensibilities, his sense of the symbiotic relationship, violates the rules he plays by. Their constant advocacy of legalization also annoys him.

138

"It is, for all intents and purposes, legal now. Possession under 30 grams is a summary conviction, no prints, no mug shot. Getting caught trafficking with even a few pounds has no real consequence beyond a fine, maybe. When you bring small-time growing operations before judges they're insulted, like we're wasting their time. What else do you want?" he says.

Clay is most fustrated with the judiciary, who he says are responsible for the situation as it stands. He says that local judges have waged war on police and their credibility.

"First of all, these guys refuse to enforce the law, to impose reasonable penalties for the crimes regarding marijuana. They essentially remove any deterrent to committing the crime because there are no consequences. It demoralizes cops, they feel they aren't being supported. It's like, 'What's the fucking point?'

"But that isn't enough for some of these guys. They have to question the integrity of police officers on the stand and in their decisions. That's not right," he says.

The Charter of Rights and Freedoms is being used by defendants, lawyers and judges to kick the snot out of cops, in Clay's opinion.

"I can't use power usage in a warrant without corroborating evidence. I can't wander around a property and listen for fans or smell for dope, look for covered windows. In many places, having a cop wander around the neighborhood looking around is considered a good thing. If you're not doing anything wrong, you don't have a problem."

Until the laws are changed, either to impose serious penalties for dope use or to decriminalize it, Clay will continue to fight the battles he thinks he can win, while doing the bare minimum fighting the war he knows is lost.

"My hope is to raise a generation of kids who won't want dope. If people don't want it, then there's no reason to grow it, is there?

139

16

The Big Bad Americans

The only thing universally feared by the dope grower, trafficker or smoker is getting caught in the United States of America. Our neighbors to the south, the founders of the legendary War on Drugs, are increasingly apoplectic about the quantity of drugs flowing across the border from British Columbia into the western states of Washington, Idaho and Montana. According to the U.S. Border Patrol, they seized 950 kilograms of marijuana from October 1, 1999, through July 31, 2000 — over double the amount seized in 1999 and over ten times the amount seized as late as 1997. Part of the reason for this increase is the growing river of pot flowing south and the rest of it is due to a concerted effort to tighten up the border and send a message to B.C.: Your dope isn't welcome here. Get caught and you will be punished.

But how do you catch them? The great undefended border is a sign of the cozy relationship between the two countries, but it poses a great difficulty in catching drug traffickers. As always, intelligence plays a key role. Word of drug shipments coming down or cash coming up sometimes leaks out, either through undercover operations down south or through informants looking for favors, or busted growers trying to get a free pass. Both the RCMP and the NCP regularly squeeze caught growers for information on their contacts in exchange for leniency. In the rare cases where a time, date and location is specified, couriers often find state cops or Border Patrol agents waiting for them.

There have also been reports — which the police agencies refuse to confirm or deny — that high-traffic areas such as decommissioned logging roads or trails through the bush are littered with sensors that are activated by weight. The sensor, often buried in the dirt road or under leaves, sends a signal back to the nearest enforcement station. The cops then make a beeline for the nearest interception point.

The border patrol has also installed state-of-the art spy cameras along a 50-kilometer stretch of the border south of Vancouver. Fiber-optic cables will be hooked up to 28 cameras, which are then to be monitored in the control room of the Border Patrol office. The $5-million project has day-and-night capability. Though this project does not yet affect Kootenay traffic, it does concern growers and couriers.

Crossing the American border through normal crossings has already become a harrowing experience for any citizen, particularly at the four crossings in the Nelson area. The almost limitless power wielded by U.S. Border Patrol agents in interrogation, search and seizure can make crossing very difficult.

There are literally hundreds of people with stories of rough treatment by U.S. Customs agents.

Dmitro, a 64-year-old Nelsonite, is one of those. He tried to cross into Washington state at the Nelway border crossing on April 15, 2000, when he was stopped by U.S. Border Patrol agents. They asked him to pull his 1968 Volvo station wagon over.

"OK, we know you have drugs and money in the car," one of the officers said. "You give it up now and we won't tear apart your car. We'll go easy on you."

"But I don't have any drugs," he said.

"Have you ever smoked marijuana?" the officer asked.

"Maybe a year ago was the last time," Dmitro said.

"Right. Listen, tell us who your guy is in the bush and we'll end this quickly."

"What? I don't know anybody like that."

"OK."

The U.S. agents proceeded to search his car, finding a pair of scissors and about $400 in cash, proof they said, of his involvement in the drug business. Dmitro says he was taken inside the border patrol station, stripped and searched in the most unpleasant ways. He was questioned for four and a half hours about his involvement in the drug trade, which he constantly and repeatedly denied. His personal papers, including an address book, bank statements and correspondence, were seized and photocopied. He was denied access to a washroom.

His car was searched thoroughly. Panels on the inside of his doors were pried off with a screw driver; his glove compartment was emptied and its contents strewn on the floor. The floor mats were torn up, the rear seats taken out. The agents found nothing.

After the search and interrogation was complete, Dmitro was denied access to the U.S. No reason was given, nor is one required. He was simply told he was not welcome in the U.S. and sent back up the road to Canada. No apology was ever offered.

Dmitro's experience is very common, according to those who live in the area. He fit the profile of those who are most commonly hassled: he has long hair and a scruffy look and he drives an older, rugged vehicle commonly used for drug transportation. Though they officially deny it, border patrol officers make no bones that are trying to make crossing the border unpleasant for some folks.

"If you're a long-haired hippy driving a shitbox, odds are I'm looking at you," says one agent. "Most of the traffickers fit a certain profile, so why wouldn't we try and target them?"

Even Const. Clay in Nelson acknowledges a certain bias in this regard.

"If some young guy is driving a Land Cruiser covered in mud, but he doesn't have any bikes or anything, I've got to wonder what he's doing in the bush," he says.

144

Cops on both sides of the border often use the dilapidated condition of the vehicles as an excuse to pull people over and then search them for marijuana.

"I got pulled over in Idaho," says one Nelsonite. "Me and some buddies were going down to a music festival. The cop said he was concerned about the safety of the vehicle. Then he said he smelled dope on us and started asking all these questions, searched the car. He found a tiny roach in the ash tray. He told us to go back home to Canada or he'd bust us. Fuck them, it isn't worth it go down there anymore unless you have to."

Some growers maintain that U.S. law enforcement agents are conducting operations on Canadian soil — an obvious violation of Canadian sovereignty.

"When I got nabbed by the RCMP," says one grower, "there was this one guy who was wearing a different color uniform and different vest and gear than the other cops. He had a different gun and he was mean as a snake, yelling at me and shit, really abusive. I asked who he was and nobody would tell me. 'Shut the fuck up,' they said. 'None of your business.'"

Almost to a one, those that have been busted by U.S. cops say the experience was entirely unpleasant, aggressive to the point of violence, as if the point was to make the process of getting pinched as traumatic as possible, using it as a deterrent. This is a far cry from the relatively friendly experience most Kootenay growers and traffickers say they have with the RCMP.

Other outdoor growers report the presence of very distinctive black helicopters flying low over their operations — entirely different from the smaller white, blue and yellow helicopters normally associated with RCMP operations.

"This huge fucking chopper is flying like 50 feet above my crop," says one grower. "I spot it, it spots me and then it's gone in a flash. The next thing, the cops show up asking questions and I mention the chopper and they say they don't have any idea what I'm talking about. Bullshit."

There is some contradiction among Canadian police agencies when the issue of cooperation with American law enforcement arises. The RCMP's Clay says he's not aware of any operations involving U.S. officers on Canadian soil.

145

"We have a working relationship, sure. And a pretty good one too. But as to Americans working up here, their jurisdiction ends at the border," he says.

The NCP's Scalia, on the other hand, says the relationship is far more extensive than that.

"We work with U.S. police agencies. We have been involved in seminars where they've shared their techniques and strategies. I won't divulge our intelligence gathering and sharing but suffice it to say we do have a good cooperative relationship," he says.

More than that, however, Scalia says the NCP works with U.S. Customs officers on operations.

"They've worked up here. In fact we're quite happy to let them handle it at the point of apprehension because their penalties are so much more significant," he says.

Growers believe it was the mounting pressure from American law enforcement agencies and government officials that led to unprecedented numbers of grow ops being busted in the Lower Mainland during the first few months of 2000.

"Here's a question for you," says one Kootenay grower. "Who the hell is paying for all these cops all of sudden doing drug busts? And more importantly, who is going to be paying for the prosecution of all these drug cases? The B.C. government? The Feds? We hear about the backlog in the courts now, wait until all this shit gets to trial."

The answer, says this grower, is simple: it's being fueled by American interests and paid for with greenbacks.

Reports from the coast say the cops have adapted a very aggressive, physical approach to their busts — a la the Americans.

"It just never used to be this way," says one grower.

Backlash against these methods is starting to crop up. More and more, police on the coast are coming across booby-trapped grow ops, including bear traps, noxious gas and spike-triggering doorways.

"People are basically saying if you're going to take me hard, then I'm going to make it hard for you," says one grower.

In the Kootenays that kind of setup is non-existent. Clay says while he's come across plenty of devices designed to alert growers to the presence of cops or that their crops have been disturbed, he's never seen anything designed to hurt a cop.

"That's just not done around here," he says.

Lower Mainland police have gone out of their way to blame the insurgence of grow ops on organized crime and Chinese gangs. Those in the industry say that while that may be true in some cases, the majority of those operations are still of the mom and pop variety.

"They don't make such a big deal about busting a 50-year-old couple because the public doesn't see it as a threat. The only way to maintain public support is to blame it on the Asian gangs," says one grower.

Still, growers in the Kootenays live in constant fear of a Lower Mainland–style, American-driven crackdown. While the border has already tightened up considerably, the invasion of cops has yet to appear.

Some growers think those in their industry who insist on exporting to the States are to blame for the heat coming down on Western Canadian pot producers.

"Greed is pushing people to the States," says a grower. "But if people would be satisfied with the little bit less money they get in Canada, we wouldn't have these problems."

There seems to be little question that the central reason American law enforcement has taken such a great interest in Canadian pot is because so much of it is ending up within their borders. Canadian pot in Canada doesn't concern them in the least. But until growers stop sending it stateside or Canadian cops get a handle on it, the U.S. seems determined to exert whatever enforcement they can.

147

Scalia for one hopes that the Americans do succeed in pressuring the Canadian government into enforcing and toughening the drug laws.

"One remedy down the line is that enough political pressure will be brought to bear by the U.S. that our governments will have another look at this so we can tackle this problem," he says.

Even Clay suggests that with more manpower he would do more.

"If they gave me a hundred cops and six months, I'd love to see what we could accomplish."

17

The Industry

Marijuana advocates talk extensively about the "underground economy" and its benefits to the Nelson area. But how realistic is this, how much money is it really worth and how does it work?

An Associated Press story in April of 2000 put the value of British Columbia's pot industry at approximately $4 billion a year. The Kootenays, it is estimated, generates anywhere from 7 to 20 per cent of this amount — an extraordinary portion when you consider that the Kootenays makes up only 3 per cent of the province's population.

First of all, a quick math lesson and some terminology: Drug dealers and dope smokers are Imperial people, meaning they speak in ounces and pounds, not in the metric equivalent of grams. Only the courts talk in grams. The most common weights for pot buyers and street level sellers are eighths, quarters and halfs. This refers to ounces, as in an eighth of an ounce, a quarter of an ounce and so on. Just for fun or the record, there are 7 grams in a quarter of an ounce and one ounce is 28 grams — exactly two grams under the 30 gram limit that results in a summary possession conviction.

Now, marijuana is affected by the same economic factors as everything else: quantity, supply and demand, that type of thing. For example, the smaller the quantity of sale, the more expensive the bud, relatively speaking. For example, using Kootenay prices, a quarter (a quarter of a ounce) will cost you $50. It will produce maybe 20 to 30 average-sized joints. A half an ounce costs $100, an ounce $200, and so on. Discounts for buying in bulk begin at four ounces, or a quarter pound.

These prices, however, are non-friend prices, you-called-me-and-you-need-some-now-prices. But this is the Kootenays and the supply is extensive, so much so that it has made the street level dealer obsolete. Most who use marijuana in this community on a regular basis either grow it themselves or know several people that do. Paying for it, or paying full pop for it, is not common among locals.

Now outside the area, marijuana is a hell of a lot more expensive. The rest of B.C. is moderately more expensive, but once you get outside the province the value rises substantially, to as much as double what Nelsonites would pay. Again the laws of supply and demand take hold.

With those basic numbers in mind, it's easy to see that a little bud goes a long way. People who are looking to only smoke what they grow can easily get by with just a few plants, and just a few more, sold discreetly to your friends, can put a new set of speakers in your hands, or whatever other modest acquisition you may have in mind.

Now on a larger scale, the numbers are a bit different. the sale price in pounds is almost strictly determined by the quality and the demand for that particular weed. B.C. bud, and Kootenay marijuana in particular, enjoys a fantastic reputation; it's the Cuban cigar of the dope world. Why? Because the people that grow it in this area love it, they worship it, they are proud of it. There is a sense of pride in the quality and the craftsmanship, the care with which it is made.

Around these parts, a pound of marijuana will sell for two grand, at the very minimum. Most times it runs between $2500 and $3500. Remember, an ounce sells for between $200 and $300 depending on the market. Grower sells for $2500, dealer sells for at least $3200. Everybody does well.

Where the numbers really get out of hand is when the dope is exported south. Four grand U.S. a pound is the generally accepted going rate. The demand for quality product in the United States is so high that the value really skyrockets. There have even been reported instances where Kootenay Gold has been traded straight up for equal amounts of cocaine. The principal reason for this is that the majority of imported marijuana coming into the U.S. is from Mexico, where the quality is substantially lower. Typically, Mexican marijuana has 5 per cent THC — the ingredient that makes people high — while Kootenay weed has a THC content akin to 20 to 25 and sometimes as high as 35 per cent.

151

These numbers come from talking to a variety of cops, growers, couriers and sellers, and everything is approximate. But the point is that this marijuana is the good stuff and is worth an astounding amount of money.

18

Cases in Point

Chris Rain grew dope in the Slocan Valley for several years. He was a large-scale, big-time grower with a sophisticated operation. He made a lot of money before getting caught.

He started, he says, because he became afflicted with Chronic Fatigue Syndrome and couldn't work any longer. He had been a handyman and general contractor for many years up until then, and without the benefit of insurance or Worker's Compensation benefits, he still needed to find a way to make a living.

He had grown a little dope before, many years ago, and mostly outdoors, so he had a general understanding of how things worked. He did a little reading — culling information from the Internet and from books that were available.

Rain also had a friend who grew a little bit and gave him some tips on how to get going and what problems to expect. After six or eight months of trial and error with various plants, Rain felt ready to try something larger.

Using his skills as a handyman he was able to turn a large underground room beneath the carport into a grow op of enviable proportions. He separated the room into four smaller enclaves and in each installed the troughs, lights, electrical equipment, timers, water pumps and ventilation systems necessary to produce weed.

He started each room in three-to four-month intervals so that every six weeks or so he could produce three to four pounds of marijuana. He would harvest it, dry it and package it for transport.

"It was a beautiful experience," says Rain. "Nurturing something from a seed to a fully grown, flowering plant is something to behold."

Once the bud was ready to go, Rain had another friend in the valley who looked after selling the product.

"I didn't want to deal with that part of it," he says. "Too dangerous, too stressful. I'd known this guy for a long time, we were friends and I trusted him." Rain says.

Rain was willing to take less than the market price to safely sell his weed. His source paid him anywhere from $1800 to $2200 a pound depending on market conditions. "It wasn't some clandestine drug deal like you see on TV. He came over, had a beer, dropped an envelope on the table and left with a garbage bag of well-packaged weed. It was very friendly."

And lucrative. Rain figures he was taking in $6,000 to $7,000 every six weeks to two months — close to $100,000 a year, tax free. He used the money to buy better equipment, but there was a lot left over so he invested it discreetly. No large-scale purchases, no fancy cars, just a nice comfortable living. It went on for over three years.

Despite the money and the enjoyment he got from tending to his plants, Rain says there was always that fear he'd get caught. He had a wife and a stepson and though they were aware of what he was doing during all those hours in the carport, he worried about what getting nabbed might mean for them.

"It's always in the back of your mind, what if... the idea of going to prison isn't very attractive," he says.

Rain's worst fears were realized one spring afternoon.

"I had a baby monitor set up outside the carport so I could hear what was going on. All of a sudden the dog starts going berzerk. I also had a little contraption so I could see what was going on above and I looked out and the place was covered with cops," he says.

The only thing was, they couldn't find him. "The carport looks completely normal from the top and you have to look around to the switch that opens the hydraulic lift to the basement. They seemed to know it was there, but couldn't find their way in," he says.

155

Rain sat tight as the cops moved about the property, his panic slowly subsiding. After about a half-hour of waiting, he became resigned to the fact that he was about to get caught. He decided to give up when an RCMP starting smashing things in the carport in an attempt to find the entranceway. He popped the door open and called out:

"Hello up there," he said.

"Well hello," said the cop who leaned over the doorway.

"I'll come up if you like," Rain said.

"OK," said the officer. He would later describe the grow room and its cloaking devices as "something out of James Bond."

Once outside the carport the cop asked him if there was anything down there he should be worried about — booby traps for instance.

"Nothing to be worried down there unless you're allergic to marijuana," Rain said.

The cop laughed.

On the way back to the house, the cop walking with Rain asked him a question: "This is all you, right?"

"What do you mean?"

"I mean, you did all this by yourself, right? Your wife and kid weren't involved were they?"

"No sir, they weren't."

"That's what I thought," said the officer.

Rain would reflect on that exchange later. "My lawyer said I shouldn't have said anything, but I just think the cop was being decent about the whole thing. He was giving me a chance to take the whole thing on myself and get my family out of it. I was really grateful for that." Rain's wife and kid were never charged.

Rain himself also beat the rap in the end. The police had received an anonymous letter from the Slocan Valley Concerned Citizens, indicating that a grow operation was taking place at Rain's residence.

"We are concerned," one letter said in part, "because people like this are growing marijuana that's being sold to our kids and they aren't paying any taxes."

Regardless of the letters' accuracy, the fact that they were unsigned made them inadmissible in court. Though confidential informants are permitted by law, the police must know the identity of the informant — in this case they claimed they didn't know who Slocan Valley Concerned Citizens were.

This wasn't the first time such a letter had appeared — in fact, for a period the SVCC were gaining a reputation as the tattlers in the valley — but their identity remains a mystery. One theory — shared by Rain — is that the SVCC is the creation of the police, a way for them to legitimize information they aren't able to confirm otherwise: a tip they can't confirm, an informant that refuses to go the distance. Either way, the judge in Rain's case threw out the letters.

The second piece of evidence used against Rain was his power records which showed that he was consuming inordinately high amounts of power. But, his lawyer argued, that in itself is not evidence of a crime.

"What if I was running my own welding business, or using lots of power tools? What if I was growing cherry tomatoes instead of marijuana?" he said.

The judge agreed, throwing out the power records too. No informant letters, no power records, no probable cause, no search warrant, no case.

The RCMP rattled their sabers for a while, talking about investigating some of Rain's property holdings as proceeds of crime, but that too went away and Chris Rain escaped scot-free.

He did give up growing up dope though.

"I'm getting older and my wife was pretty freaked out by the experience. The whole thing of not knowing what's going to happen was hard on the family. If I was a younger man..."

Chris Rain has since left the Slocan Valley, off, as they say, to less greener pastures.

Matt and Brigit Stevens have day jobs. Matt works as a logger and Brigit works as a secretary in a busy office. They live on the North Shore, on an acre and a half property a few kilometers from Nelson on which they discreetly grow a few marijuana plants at the back of their garden. The plot of land that holds the pot is shielded from the road by a few trees. Each year in the fall their plants produce close to ten pounds of good green bud, which they dry in their basement. Their main reason for doing it is simple: it's cheaper than buying product.

"We used to buy close to a quarter a week," says Brigit, who admits that she and Matt smoke up pretty much every night. "Even around here it was getting pretty expensive. A friend of ours had some extra seeds, we had some space in the garden..."

Brigit and Matt keep a good portion of their dope for themselves, seal it up tight and then freeze it in their deep freezer in their basement.

"It's not as strong after it's been frozen, but it still works good," she says with a little giggle.

The rest of their stash they sell to friends on the side, a quarter or a half an ounce at a time — never more than that.

"We're not drug dealers," says Brigit. "We provide a service for our friends. Matt's work is seasonal so during the winter making the truck payment is sometimes tough. Honest extra money helps".

Brigit says that once the dope is gone for the year, it's gone.

"Sometimes people get dry and ask us for some and we have to say no. We have our personal stuff and we don't dip into that — otherwise we end up paying for it again, which defeats the purpose."

Brigit says they've resisted the urge to go bigger with their operation, simply because they don't want to get in trouble and jeopardize their normal jobs. They're small-time growers and they intend to stay this way. She dismisses the idea that's she doing anything wrong.

"We're not hurting a single soul with what we're doing here. And let's face it, we're hardly the only ones doing this around here."

Sara Samuels was a teacher in one of the small satellite communities outside of Nelson. She taught grade school kids.

Samuels was from the Lower Mainland and got her teaching degree at the University of Victoria. It was, she says, all she ever wanted to do it.

That, and raise her daughter in a good home. During her third year in college she had a fling with a grad student from a South American country. He was handsome and thoughtful and after she got pregnant and he graduated, he bolted as fast he could back to his native land, never to be heard from again. Sara didn't really mind. Her daughter was a joy.

But there was no question that parenting made for tough financial times. As a rookie teacher in a small community the wages were not always enough to cover the expenses. She had a car loan, rent and a heavy student debt load, not to mention the expenses associated with having a young child — day care, strollers, cribs, high chairs — the list went on and on.

Struggling to make ends meet, Sara decided to grow some dope in the basement of her rented home. She knew a guy who did it and he helped her get set up in a small, windowless storage room. A couple of lights was all she needed to grow enough marijuana to make things easier on her and her daughter.

159

She sold none of her weed on the local market, petrified of getting caught. She still had friends at the Uiniversity of Victoria, one of whom was a regular pot smoker. For a little bud, he set her up with his contact. The initial meeting was a little nervewracking, but it turned out she knew the dealer from a class she had taken, so it was no big deal. The dealer was happy to get a source of good quality Kootenay Gold from someone he could trust.

So every three months or so, Sara would pack up her Toyota Tercel for a weekend trip to Vancouver Island. Included in her suitcase would be a couple of pounds of carefully packaged marijuana, and some Oso Negro coffee, locally produced java that smelled strong and tasted like a yummy hand grenade.

She got her friends on the island to buy that too. Sometimes her daughter would come along, sometimes she'd stay with the sitter. It was a long drive, but it was worth it because each time she'd come back with somewhere in the neighborhood of $5,000. Not a gargantuan sum by any means, but certainly enough to make life a little easier. It was nice to get away and see her friends on the coast as well.

One spring evening, Sara noticed some water leaking into her basement. It wasn't much and it was on the other side from her little bud room. Still she was worried about what damage it might cause, so she called her landlord.

Mr. Gardener came over to look at the water accumulating in a small pool in the basement. He decided it was nothing to worry about, just typical spring runoff. He told Sarah just to sweep it into the storm drain in the center of the floor every now and again.

"There should be a broom in the storage room in the corner," he said. "Why don't you get it and we'll do it now."

"Actually the broom's right over there," Sara said, her heart climbing into her throat.

"Oh. OK." Mr. Gardener grabbed it and proceeded to sweep the water away. When he was finished he put the broom back and then glanced over at the storage room.

"Sara, is there a reason there is a lock on the storage room door?" he asked.

"Yeah, sorry, I just had some valuables that I wanted to make sure didn't get nabbed. A bike and stuff, you know," Sara's heart was thundering, she was sure he'd hear it.

Mr. Gardener didn't bat an eye. "OK then," he said.

After Mr. Gardener left, Sara spent a sleepless night worrying about what had happened. Should she ditch the marijuana in the room? Would he rat her out? He seemed like a nice old guy, she figured in the end, he probably didn't even give it a second thought.

Six months later, Sara was heading down Highway 3A just outside of Nelson on her way to Victoria when an RCMP cruiser appeared behind her and turned on his bubble lights. She knew right away that she'd been busted. She was glad her daughter was at the sitter's.

The cops were pleasant enough at first, but got increasingly mean. They gave her a very tough choice: tell them about her connections and they'd make the charges against her a painless as possible — maybe even go away. They threatened to involve Child and Family Services, and Sara broke down in tears. But she couldn't give up her friends — that would just make matters worse.

They charged Sara with trafficking, she pleaded guilty and paid a small fine and received a short period of probation. The judge seemed sympathetic. She never got a call from Child and Family Services. She did, however, lose her job as a teacher. Her principal called her in one day and said he'd been informed by a parent of one of the students — he didn't say who — that she'd been convicted of trafficking. He was sorry, but the school board frowned on teachers as dope growers.

161

Sara packed up her things and left Nelson to look for other work. She was heading East, trying to get as far away from her conviction as possible, unsure if her record would follow her wherever she went.

She hoped not.

Gary Bergvall is a man who turned what he learned during his career as a marijuana manufacturer into a viable, profitable — and perfectly legal — business. Bergvall is one of the co-owners of Kootenay Growers Supply, now at two locations to serve you.

Bergvall sells the equipment any enterprising botanist needs to start his or her very own hydroponic pot operation.

For between four and five thousand dollars, Bergvall sells prefab units that include everything a budding bud grower needs: lights, troughs, electrical supplies, timers, pumps — essentially a turnkey grow op.

"Most people that come in here have done enough reading to know what they're getting into. It's not as if you can just throw some seeds into a pot, flip the switch and presto, instant pot. It's a bit more complicated than that," says Bergvall.

At the same time, he emphasizes that even the brownest of the green thumbs can usually get something going.

"It is, after all, a weed. Just leave the fucking thing alone and let nature take its course," he says.

Bergvall is no-nonsense kind of guy with a long pony tail, square jaw and the occasional wad of chew in his lip. He does not mess about.

"Some guys come in here wanting to talk about growing dope, but I tell them I can't help them. Now if you want to talk about growing plants — be they vegetables or flowers or even weeds if you really want to — then I can probably help you," says Bergvall with a slight smile.

He admits freely, however, that probably 80 per cent of his business comes from people growing dope in their basements. Kootenay Growers now employs eight people with stores in Nelson and on the North Shore, about 10 minutes outside Nelson.

Aside from selling premade kits — which are also available online — Bergvall designs and manufactures custom electrical equipment. Most indoor grow ops require a substantial power supply and an industrial electrical outlet — like the ones that stoves are plugged into. The lights, pumps and timers, however, generally run off a three-prong plug. Bergvall has created a power converter that can run the whole show. It meets all

Canadian Standard Association safety requirements and Bergvall is exporting them to the U.S. He has great contempt for growers that jury rig their power supplies, either because they don't know any better or because they are trying to get out of paying the substantial power bill that growing requires.

"Those people are putting themselves and their entire neighborhoods at risk," he says. "Do it right and pay the power bill. They're giving you the power, why shouldn't you pay for it?" he says.

Just after Bergvall started the store almost four years ago he got a call at work. It was the RCMP telling him they had a search warrant for his house, could he please come home.

"I told them I didn't want to but I would," he says. "I got there, walked right to the cop and shook his hand and they went ahead and did their business."

What they found was "one the most sophisticated grow ops ever built." It was so well put together that it actually helped beat the charge. The police officer testified that he could smell marijuana even while standing off the property 50 feet from the house. The RCMP's own pictures of the operation showed state of the art aerosol sprayers and odor maskers that would have made it impossible to smell the marijuana upstairs in the kitchen, never mind outside the house on the road. Case dismissed.

163

By that time Bergvall was starting to have some success with the store and having fun developing a line of products he could as be proud of as his other product — but that wouldn't run him afoul of the law.

"Besides, the store just made me such an obvious target, it would be kind of stupid to grow dope as well," he says. He claims that since his bust the cops haven't hassled him at all.

Bergvall is in a unique position to observe the pot-growing industry in Nelson — almost everybody buying products from him is doing it. Bergvall says that the stereotypical dope grower with the long hair, stinking at patchouli oil, talking like Cheech and Chong, is a myth.

"There are some of those guys, sure, but most people that do this are just regular folks doing their thing in private. They're young, old, with day jobs, moms, dads, wives, whatever. There is no profile that fits. It's everywhere, it's everyone," he says.

Bergvall says the industry is by and large a very friendly one, where rip-offs are rare and everyone gets along just fine. The dirty stuff happens far away and several steps removed from the Kootenays.

"Most people here aren't really interested in getting rich, they're just trying to make their lives a little better. They go on vacation or worry less about their mortgage. Most of them aren't involved in the transport and especially not the sale of their product. They know a guy and he knows a guy and he knows guy that's a Hell's Angel and he has buddies that work for a trucking company. But that's a long ways away from Mom and Dad's basement, you know what I'm saying?"

Bergvall insists that most people grow pot because it is, at its root, an enjoyable experience that is profitable too.

164

"You put these seeds down, you water them, give them light, love them and they flower and bloom and produce this wonderful smell and this great substance. You take pride in it. It can be an almost spiritual experience.

This is a sentiment shared by many a dope grower — that love is they key to creating great dope. Many believe that dope grown expressly for greedy purposes will not perform nearly as well as dope grown for the "right" reasons.

"I went in on this outdoor crop with this other guy one time," says Pete, another Kootenay grower. "He was desperate for the things to flower so he could make his money. Almost every day he was up there on the mountain almost choking the shit out these plants yelling, 'Grow you sonafabitches, grow!' It was one of the lousiest crops I've ever had because it wasn't treated right."

Bergvall agrees that greedy dope growers can make things tough on the whole industry.

"These guys that are trying to make a fast buck, exporting to the States, moving huge quantities — they're taking huge risks and they're drawing way too much attention to themselves and subsequently the whole deal. Take it easy and things will work out for all of us."

Decriminalization of small grow ops is something Bergvall thinks would be good for the country — and good for him. He believes the amount of time, energy and money wasted on something as innocuous as marijuana is laughable. He also thinks that further relaxed laws would help business.

"I think a lot more people would buy home grow outfits if it wasn't against the law and the last remaining stigmas of law-breaking were taken away. Some people still look both ways before walking out of here — but not many."

Bergvall walks out of his store every day with his head held high.

165

Tim Charles looks like a middle-aged hippy. In his mid-thirties, with long, generally greasy hair and scruffy goatee, Charles is a ten-year veteran of the Kootenay marijuana scene and an experienced outdoor grower. He has dabbled with hydroponic weed, but finds it unappealing, like many of his friends and associates.

"Here in Nelson, because of the health consciousness, outdoor marijuana is very appealing. Generally you can be a lot more sure that the soil's healthier, just because of the fact that the chemical fertilizers used in many hydroponic operations can be deadly. Most people around here don't smoke 'indoor,' they prefer pure, organic bud," he says.

As with all outdoor weed, Charles grows only one crop a year, usually on a piece of Crown land deep in the bush. He and his friends plant the crop in the late spring or early summer and harvest it in the fall. They visit their plants periodically, tending to them the best they can. Outdoor weed, according to Charles, is usually of the Cannabis sativa variety, whereas Cannabis indica is used indoor because of the shorter grow cycle.

Because of his connections in the community, Charles uses only seed strains that he is familiar with or that come highly recommended. He says attention to this detail, by both indoor and outdoor growers, is the key to the area's reputation for spectacular weed.

"It's not so much the bud, but the line that it came from. There's Kootenay pedigree, lines that have been grown here for up to 20 years," says Charles, mentioning the "J" strain and "Ken's Super Sativa" as just two of the many well-preserved seed strains in the area. He says that the Doukhobours, who grew marijuana as multi-purpose substance, have some of the best, fastest-growing strains around. "A lot of people that don't know what they're doing are always getting new seed stock, and they have no idea where it came from. But around here there is a pride," he says.

166

"Kootenay Green" enjoys a reputation in Oregon, Florida and California, where it is known for its distinct smell and wheel-chair THC levels.

The downside to growing outdoors is that it exists in a less controlled environment that is accessible to everyone. "A lot of people's crops get stolen off the hills," says Charles.

"There are people that come up here specifically in the months of September and October and they traverse down the mountain sides. Some of these patches can be worth $50,000 or $60,000, just laying there like a big pile of gold," he says.

Despite that, Charles says there is very little violence related to outdoor growing. Few people have the time or inclination to guard a crop well into the bush, and would be unable or unwilling to be violent should the situation arise anyway. Charles has had his crop stolen only once in 10-plus years of outdoor growing.

The only violence Charles is aware of comes from people that do not follow his spiritually oriented pursuit of marijuana and are involved in the hard drugs that Charles never has and never will deal with.

"The only exception [to violence] would be on the East Shore and parts of the Valley where there is a lot of cocaine and people tend to trade their crop for powder drugs. There's this weird scene where people just grow it and trade it and then do a bunch of coke for a month and then it's over. That's the closest thing to violence that I've seen," he says.

Growing outdoor pot is also safer when it comes to enforcement. With RCMP resources at a premium, he figures the odds of the RCMP dispatching officers to search the mountains for marijuana or pay the cost of running helicopter surveillance are slim. It also helps that, unlike indoor grow ops on private property, most outdoor is planted on Crown land.

167

"The only way you can bust someone growing outdoor pot is them having a big sack of pot after the fact. I could be standing there watering a patch on Crown land and boom the cops pop up and I'm busted. But I'm saying, 'I didn't know what that was. I was hiking and I came upon them and they looked dry and there was a creek right there...' The cops will say, 'You expect us to believe that?' But do you have a video camera that shows me planting it? Even if I was harvesting it, there's always the claim that I didn't know what it was."

Even if caught, Charles says it's been his experience that it's extremely unlikely a person would go to jail for growing, even on their second offense. "Most people I know don't even worry about getting caught," he says. "Most cops don't care unless someone brings it to their attention, and even then there is no guarantee that it will lead to big trouble.

"We had a situation where an RCMP officer came to a guy's house where we were growing in a greenhouse and he said, 'Look, we're getting reports that you've got plants practically coming through the ceiling of your greenhouse and you're making it a bit too obvious. We're going to be back in two hours and we want to see that empty'. We made a phone call and made a bunch of oil right away. The cops gave us an opportunity, they were basically saying, 'Let's just avoid the headache.'"

There is no stigma in the community either.

"I think it's generally accepted in the community that you have to do something worse than grow pot to be labelled as a bad person. I think it's almost honorable. I think that's why the government changed the charge in the Controlled Drugs and Substances Act from "Cultivation of Cannabis Marijuana" to "Production of a Controlled Substance" because it sounded too honorable. You weren't anybody in Nelson until you had your cultivation badge. It sounded so benign," he says.

Charles and his friends try to grow it in enough quantity to last them for a year, selling whatever extra they have to friends or maybe taking a little to the coast for some extra cash. They never export their product to the U.S. He thinks that marijuana for export creates many of the problems associated with the industry. He knows commercial growers, but does not hang with them.

"There are two distinct groups here, one that is exporting to the States and one that is growing for personal pleasure. I've always dealt with the personal pleasure group, but I do know the other group. They seem really greedy," he says.

In Charles's mind, marijuana for profit leads to crappy marijuana. "You can't grow it thinking, 'This plant's a VCR, this plant's a payment on my boat.' It never works. There really is a spiritual aspect to it in order to get to a level of bud that you would have pride in. It's a spiritual thing, it's almost a joke how much it's worth."

The people to whom Kootenay marijuana is worth the most are American drug dealers. Its quality is far superior to any other import with THC levels four to five times as high. Marijuana from the Caribbean or Central America is hard to import and the growers in those arid climates are more inclined to grow hard drugs anyway. There is some domestically produced marijuana, but because the federal penalties for cultivating and transporting marijuana are so high, ganja growers in the U.S. run a great risk of doing serious federal pen time — something everybody agrees is not appealing. The several hundred thousand dollars a year a grower can make is not worth risking 15 years in a 12' by 12' cell.

169

Canada poses none of those difficulties. The penalties for growing and moving even large quantities of bud are relatively inconsequential when compared to those imposed under U.S. law. In B.C. in particular, the penalties are notoriously light, in Nelson even more so. In addition, the border between Canada and the U.S.A. is often referred to as "the longest undefended border in the world" and while that does speak well for the diplomatic relationship between the two countries, it also makes it easier to move drugs and money across the border.

For Kootenay growers, the vast majority of which are not in any way interested in trying to move their product across the border themselves, there are two ways to get their crop south of the border where the prices are substantially higher than what is paid locally or even in other parts of Canada.

The first is to let the Americans come to you. Growers maintain that every few months or so an American dealer will come to the area and put the word out that he's looking for product.

"There are buyers that come here, much like the old tobacco purchasers with wads of American money. A lot of the deals go down behind closed doors with an intermediary," says one grower.

In the relatively small network of growers, word gets around who's got crop ready, and connections are made. It happens in a very easy way, according to those involved.

"It's all very friendly," says another person involved. "Rip-offs are extremely, extremely rare and violence is non-existent. Everybody wants to maintain a good reputation and be able to come back. There's enough money to go around."

The second way to access the American market is to conscript the services of a locally based courier. These men are generally considered to be the highest-risk takers in the industry because it's their job to carry large quantities of marijuana across the border and either make the transaction for cash, or leave the marijuana at a specified drop point. In some cases they also must bring cash, and in some rare cases hard drugs, back across the border.

"Those are the really crazy guys," says a grower.

170

19

The Bad Craziness of Couriers

Steve Roberts stopped his snowmobile 200 feet from the four wheel drive pick up that was parked on the old logging road just inside the U.S. border. He peered through the blue-white light of the setting sun glinting off the snow. Something didn't feel quite right.

His buddy Garth Wallace stopped his snowmobile and came up beside Steve. They both flipped up the visors on their helmets so they could speak to each other easily.

"What's up?" asked Garth.

"I'm not sure. You think that's the truck Billy would be driving?" Steve motioned to the old, rusty Ford with King Kong–sized winter tires.

"I dunno," Garth shrugged under his heavy snowmobile suit. The truck was running but the two of them couldn't see anyone inside.

It was supposed to be an easy trip: zip over the border, pick up some jingle and boogie back home to Canada. No 50 pounds of dope to lug around, just several hundred thousand quon, dineros, greenbacks to pick up and deliver safely back home to the King.

Billy, the American contact, was supposed to have the money ready at this spot at this time, but something didn't feel quite right to Steve. Billy was a good guy who partied a little too hard and spent a little too much money, but he was the King's main driver and that was that.

"Well, fuck," said Steve.

"Nothing to do now, man. Might as well check it out," said Garth. They fired up the sleds and moved forward off the trail they'd followed from Canada onto the logging road. As they got closer, Steve realized it wasn't Billy in the cab of the truck, but some shiteater, backwater sheriff, who hopped out of the cab, shotgun in hand, and started yelling at them.

172

They had a second to decide: spin the sleds and make a break for it — and maybe get shot in the process — or stop and get pinched.

The sheriff lifted the gun up and Steve eased off the throttle. He and Garth stopped and shut off the sleds. They could hear what Sgt. Hick was shouting now.

"Get on the ground, motherfuckers!"

And so they did.

Steve Roberts doesn't really want to talk about this. Well, he sort of doesn't. He doesn't want make trouble for himself or his friends. And the people he's been dealing with are not the type of folks you screw around with, you know what I'm saying? It's not that they'd kill him, or even break his legs — well *probably* not — but it is just unwise to be telling stories about stuff that nobody talks about out of school.

On the other hand ... well, it's a great life, isn't it? It's got an almost action movie quality to it, and bragging about beating the keystone cops and judicifool system is something that's altogether too tempting.

Roberts has been hemming and haaaing about this for weeks. He moves around quite a bit and, uh, he travels a lot, so he's hard to pin down. Finally, he's on the phone — "Are you sure this thing's secure?" — and ready to talk.

Roberts came to the Nelson area in 1994 from points east to try out the legendary powder. He had a few years of university under his belt, but no real focus, so he simply dropped out, packed up what he could and hitched to B.C. Soon he fell into a crowd that was doing exactly what he wanted to do: making enough money to live a recreational-oriented, party-dominated life.

173

Most of his new friends — 20-somethings with a crazy streak — were involved in the dope trade in some way. They either grew it, moved it across the border or drove it from the U.S. side to its final destination anywhere in the continental U.S.

The money was absolutely ridiculous — it paid for killer sleds and kick-ass dirtbikes — and the adrenaline rush was unreal. Imagine a Mountain Dew commercial with cops and bud strapped to the bikes.

At the center of Roberts' little crowd of bandits is the King: a nice fellow in his early 30s that Roberts met only once or twice at parties. He grows no weed, makes no trips across the border, takes no chances. But the King has two things that nobody else has: huge piles of disposable cash and connections.

The King has "friends" all across the States. Criminals in the strict sense of the word, but more like buddies, guys he's met through various excursions and ventures over the years. When they need weed they simply place an order with the King. This is not dime baggies, this is major weight — anywhere from 70 to 250 pounds or "p".

The King then fills the order by going to various growers in the area and seeing what they have available. Always people he knows and trusts, always people who know and trust him. They are mom and pop operations, they are college kids, they are whoever. When he has his necessary weight together, packaged and ready for shipping, the King employs couriers, usually two, and a driver. These people always know and trust each other.

The driver crosses the border legally and sets up shop in a small town by renting a car and a hotel room. The driver would have a pre-arranged time to meet the couriers.

The couriers were responsible for getting the weed across the border and meeting the driver on the other side (this is what Roberts does). There are as many different ways to get it across the border as you can think of, according to Roberts:

By Land

In a rented cube van: taking the interior walls off the inside of the box, packing them with bud and cayenne pepper (to throw off the dogs) and replacing the walls. "They're catching on to this one, though."

In a train: crossing the border in a train — like by boat — is a less scrutinized ordeal: no X-ray machines, no definite custom searches, etc.

With the old fogies: "There's this couple I know," Steve says, "they are in their 60s and they've been going across the border for lunch every three weeks for almost ten years. They drive this old, immaculate Town Car and they look all the world like your grandma and grandpa. And every time they go they are carrying a trunk full of marijuana. They never, ever get stopped. Ever. They even know some of the Border Patrol guards by name."

By Sea

In a boat: more common on the Coast than in the Interior, but everything from pleasure cruisers, to sailboats to sea kayaks can be packed with bud. And unlike air travel or driving across the border, going across the 49th parallel in a boat is often easier, or at least less scrutinized.

In a log: one of Roberts' favorites. "There are these guys who stuffed sealed packets of bud into a log along with a GPS [Global Positioning Satellite] beacon. Then they floated the log down a river into the States while they drove across the border. They tracked down the log, unpacked the dope and viola..."

Underwater: dive in on one side, swim across the border, climb out on the other.

By Air

In a plane: Roberts says he knows of Cessna pilots who have loaded up their planes with mary jane at small town airports or rural airports and then made their drop just over the U.S. border to a driver on the other side.

"Any way you think can think of," Roberts says, "it's been done."

Roberts' favorite way of transporting dope over the border is what he calls "bushwacking": just a couple of guys with backpacks or hockey bags or duffel bags full of weed pushing through the forest. Sometimes they follow trails, sometimes they don't. Sometimes they use dirtbikes or snowmobiles, sometimes they do it on foot. It depends where they think the Border Patrol is likely to be monitoring, where they've heard is hot, the terrain and the time of year. For example, it's difficult to use dirtbikes in the early spring because of all the mud. Snowmobiles are a necessity in February, when the snow is the deepest. The other factor is simply fun. Roberts and his cohorts enjoy the toys of the trade and on some days feel like using them.

"For six hours that backwater sheriff drove us up and down the road, saying over and over again, 'Where's the dope where's the dope where's the dope?' Roberts says. "Not, 'Where's the weed?' or 'Where's the heroin?' or 'Where's the money?' Just 'Where's the dope where's the dope where's the dope?' For six hours."

Roberts and his buddy Garth sat, handcuffed, in the cab of this truck the whole time as the sheriff drove up and down the road, occaisonally jumping out with his dog — so old that it hadn't smelled it's own pooper in 10 years — to search the bushes for the dope. Exhausted, cold and wet, the sheriff gave up as the sun came out.

Sitting in the truck, it was all so very funny to Roberts. There was, of course, no dope to be found and they figured their contact, the aforementioned Billy, was either long gone or long incarcerated by now. Still, Roberts was a little scared. Jail time in the U.S. is what scares couriers the most, and that nightmare was about to become a reality.

For the couriers the draw is the money. Well, it's also the adrenaline rush of maybe getting caught with serious weight, but mostly it's the money. Roberts' cut if he's doing the whole deal himself — delivering the weed and picking up the cash — is usually around $100 per pound. So for a few hours' work and maybe 30 minutes of real danger, he would get anywhere between $5,000 and $7,500.

"The scariest part is the 20 or so kilometers on either side of the border," Roberts says. "That's where you are at the greatest risk of getting nailed."

Once across the border, Roberts meets up with his contact, the driver. He then gives the driver the weed and immediately heads back across to the Canadian side. The driver would then head to points south — Cali, Utah, Florida — wherever the King has made his contact.

The drivers are the guys who get paid the serious cash because they take the biggest risks of all. It's a job, that for all his bravado, even Roberts shies away from. Imagine driving long distances in a car loaded down with a minimum of 100 and up to 250 pounds of high-grade Canadian ganga in the country with the highest incarceration rate in the world. Every lane change is signalled, every speed limit obeyed.

The greatest risk to drivers, as with couriers, lies close to the border. That's where Roberts got nabbed and that's where most of the drivers get nailed too.

"When you're within 30 km of the border, that's when it's the scariest. The further you get away, the more you blend back in with everyone else," says Roberts.

Drivers also have to deal with U.S. contacts on the other end and while that's usually a smooth process, there's always the danger that something could go violently wrong. Roberts says, however, that it's rare.

"The driver would know the contact, and vice-versa. There's no way you would just go down there and knock on some guy's door, 'Hi, I'm here with the weed, where's my quarter mil.?" says Roberts. "It's pretty casual. Sometimes it will take the U.S. guys a day or two to get the cash together and then you'd just hang out, go skiing, whatever. But generally it's all ready to go."

The process is the same with the cash coming back. The driver meets the couriers at an out-of-the-way location near the border. The couriers then take the money and head for home; the driver drops the rental car and returns to Canada as well.

Roberts says he's been tempted on that final leg of the journey just to dissapear with the jingle.

"You're walking through the bush with several hundred thousand quon and it crosses your mind that you could just take off," says Roberts. "You could never go back, but I doubt anybody would look too hard. It's not the mob, or some international syndicate. If you fucked off to Europe, nobody would ever find you."

But nobody ever does take off.

"It's like you'd be ripping off your buds, your brothers. Plus if all that money went missing, everybody gets hurt: drivers, Kings, couriers, mom and pop growers — it all trickles down. Everybody that's involved in this knows one another, likes each other, parties together. You just don't bring in people who would mess that up."

But it does get messed up now and again, mostly from unbridled stupidity. That's how guys get nabbed.

Roberts tells the story of one guy who ran out of gas on the interstate in California with 70 pounds of marijuana in the car. The cops came by to help out and the guy got caught.

"That's how it happens, people just being dumb," he says.

The driver's bail was $70,000, posted by the King. He then proceeded to flee back to Canada, never to return to the land of Red, White and Blue ever again. That backup, says Roberts, is essential.

"You have friends that have money and they post your bail if you get nabbed. Especially if you're a driver and you're taking the risk, you know you have friends and that you're not going to be spending the rest of life down there. You'd be taken care of, for sure," he says.

Roberts says there are no consequences for the individuals if couriers or drivers get nailed.

"It is simply the cost of doing business and everybody just sucks it up," he says.

Besides, getting caught is rare, Roberts says.

"It's rarely smart cops. It's usually somebody who should know better doing something dumb."

Billy, the driver, was doing something dumb when he got caught. Instead of using a car, Billy was bringing the jingle back to the border by train. He'd met some new friends on the train and soon they were pissed, making lots of racket, annoying other passengers, giving the conductors a hard time. At a rest stop the cops were called to deal with the rowdies and soon Billy was forced to explain what the $220,000 in U.S. currency was doing in his duffel bag. He couldn't.

Billy swears he didn't give Roberts and the other courier Garth up. The Border Patrol, during Roberts' two days of questioning in a Montana jail, said they'd heard the sleds while doing routine surveillance and radioed the sheriff for backup - that it was just bad luck that they'd been caught.

179

After two days — without a phone call — the Border Patrol admitted they'd found nothing incriminating in the area and since Roberts and Garth weren't carrying anything, there was nothing drug-related to charge them with. They were transferred to the Immigration and Naturalization Service holding prison in Seattle.

Roberts says his time in American jails was not as scary as he thought it would be. In fact, as they were local jails, the most unseemly thing Roberts encountered was drunks sleeping off their booze.

"I was kind of freaked out at first, but once I realized they didn't have anything to charge us with, it wasn't really too bad," Roberts says.

The INS jail, however, was less congenial. Packed with people facing deportation to places far less appealing than Canada, there was an air of desperation about the place. And the food was absolutely terrible.

After 13 days of incarceration, Roberts and Garth were brought before a judge, charged with entering the country illegally. The judge simply kicked them out of the country, warned them never to do it again. Two weeks after getting nabbed, they were home in Canuckville.

Meanwhile, Billy was already home by then. The U.S. government kept the money and sent him packing.

Roberts says he feels lucky to have gotten off so easy. He realizes that city lockups and INS pens aren't hard federal time. He hasn't done any dope runs since getting nabbed and says he probably won't unless he really needs the money. He says he doesn't miss the rush of the pursuit, that it isn't as exciting once you've been caught. Not that he wants people to think he's gone soft.

"Don't put that in there, that I don't want to do it anymore. Say, 'Fuckin' right, I'll do it again.'"

20

The Battlefield of Youth

What has become strikingly apparent about this running guerrilla war between the police and the Nelson establishment on one hand and the marijuana minions led by the likes of the Holy Smokers on the other, is that they both claim to be protecting the kids. For the cops and the politicians "protect the kids" is the cry they use to justify just about everything they do, from totalitarian civic bylaws to questionable searches. Most of them, in their 30s, 40s and 50s, are family people with children of their own. Part of their vitriolic attitude toward marijuana and its advocates can be directly attributed to the fact that they see their own children at risk too. For marijuana growers and users, their fight is geared toward personal freedom and challenging what they see as unjust laws. They too see it as a fight for the children, a struggle to leave their offspring with a better, more liberated world.

Between the police, the media and popular culture, North American young people are bombarded with conflicting messages about marijuana. In Nelson, where marijuana is such a major part of the daily landscape, teens are even more swamped. Gauging what teens are thinking is always a tricky prospect. But after talking to dozens of teens over a two-year period, there are some general conclusions I can draw about how teens in Nelson view the herb and the war of words surrounding it.

The first thing that is evident is that kids in the Kootenays have almost laughably easy access to marijuana. It is easier to obtain, most agree, than alcohol, especially in a small town with only three places to buy beer and one liquor store — and where the cashier is likely to be a soccer mom whose kid plays on your team.

"This is Nelson, the marijuana big time. You don't even have to try, it's everywhere," says Jane, 16, who admits she smokes up every now and then. The most common source seems to be older siblings, or friends who have friends involved in the trade. There are, the kids say, no dealers that frequent the school.

"The teachers and cops would catch on pretty quick," Jane says.

Marijuana use is so prevalent that some teens estimate usage runs in the 60 to 70 per cent range. It has very little negative stigma attached to it, even less than cigarettes, which most teens agree are a major health hazard.

"It's just accepted, it's no big deal. I don't think it's as unhealthy as drinking. In Nelson, smoking tobacco is more shunned than smoking weed," says Pete, 17. "It kills you and it doesn't do anything for you. At least there is some fun in smoking pot."

The kids also agree that programs established by the school to talk about pot, or police officers giving talks on the subject, do not have any substantial effect.

"I think the emphasis is put more on the illegal drugs than the legal drugs and that's totally bad. It's not like you can buy crack around here. It seems to me that they teach you about drugs you have never even heard about and not much about alcohol or pot."

Conversely, teenagers agree that the drinking and driving presentations leave a strong impression. "If there is one thing that people have been successful preaching to kids it's drinking and driving. Nobody I know would ever do it. Getting on the road when you're drunk, it's not just your own life you're dealing with."

The most common place teens say they consume dope — and alcohol for that matter — is at house parties, of which they say there is usually at least one every weekend and more during the summer. Of those, usually a half dozen are really good, everyone-is-there-and-bombed parties. At those parties, marijuana is as common as booze.

183

"Pretty much at every party you will find a few smoke sessions going on. People leave the party and come back . . .or just bust it out right there in the middle of the living room," says Chris, also 16. He says the potheads are rarely a problem but those who drink in excess are a constant source of confrontation, violence and property destruction.

"Let's put it this way — nobody ever gets their house trashed by some stoner."

There are, of course, a great number of students who do not partake in the herb. Most say that decision is a personal one, not influenced by outside forces, though some will admit that family experiences have led them away from substances they've seen to be problematic. Most kids who stay away from pot also stay away from booze. Those that choose abstention say the peer pressure they feel is more from the fact they are a minority than anything else.

"Where I feel the peer pressure is not with alcohol, it's with marijuana," says Mia, 15. "It's not a direct peer pressure, like 'Come on, why don't you toke.' It's just that everyone around you is doing it and you almost feel like an outsider or strange if you are not familiar with that substance. That's what has made me feel like an outsider – my opinions on marijuana because a lot of people still view it as harmless. I think people are aware of the effects of alcohol more than they are aware of the negative effects of marijuana."

Mia thinks that weed has gained a reputation through the culture in Nelson and, albeit less so, through movies, T.V. and other media.

"I think it's trendy. I think a lot of people think it's cool to smoke marijuana. I think another big part of it is the whole style and image thing. Even though it's not a stylish thing to do, there is something about it that people think is cool."

Like the marijuana scene in Nelson as a whole, the kids say it is difficult to pinpoint a certain stereotype consistent with marijuana use or even identify individuals that are heavy users. Says Sarah, 17: "It's hard to tell in this town because you just assume everyone does. Because you know them, you know the people who go out every break and smoke up. That's the only way you can really know, because somebody you would think would be a complete chronic doesn't even touch it."

All the kids agree on one thing: that parents have the strongest impact on the thinking processes and decisions made by teenagers. Some of them say they have been exposed to it by the families themselves because Mom and Dad like the occasional puff themselves. That, says one teenager who smells marijuana after she goes to bed from time to time, undermines any credibility they might have.

"Some of them can't really say anything about it because they do it too."

It's a difficult line to navigate because parents inevitably will expose their kids to alcohol. The best approach for parents seems to be to behave responsibly and hope that the kids will too. It's part of growing up. Kids are naturally curious and most are rebellious and like to challenge boundaries. Teens say that the kids who do it the most, or want to do it the most, are the ones whose parents are super strict and don't want them to do it. The kids who are told to make their own decisions approach it differently. Many teens have parents who grew up with marijuana use and accept that some experimentation is going to take place.

"I think most parents don't mind you experiencing something, they just don't want you to be hooked on it. I think the main fear about marijuana is that it will lead to other drugs," says Key, 16. "My parents get me to think really socially and critically about weighing the pros and cons. If you are a critical thinker then you can understand all sides of an issue, and once you see every side then you can make a choice. I think the best way to handle it is through education, not education saying 'Don't do drugs,' but education saying what is good about it and what is bad about it."

Rick is a teacher in an alternative school in town that deals with kids who have difficulty fitting into the traditional school system. Most of the time it's the rigidity of the structure, the discipline that kills them. They act up, act out and get kicked out. Instead of heading to the welfare rolls or some low-level job, the kids have a second chance at this particular school. It is smaller and less structured, the kids work more on their own clock. It's an alternative approach to education and it works fairly well.

But these are the "bad kids" and a lot of them smoke pot. Rick knows the kids walking into the alley behind his school are off on a Nelson-style "smoke break." There's no heavy hand here, just "Put it out and go home." One of the cardinal rules is not being stoned at school.

Rick has a fool-proof test for kids who come to school stoned. He asks them: "Are you stoned?" Inevitably those that are break into a huge, goofy-ass grin, or break up laughing. Those who aren't just look at him with this are-you-crazy-half-hurt expression.

On the issue of whether dope is a problem at his school, Rick says the question is too simple. Most of the kids that come to his school have larger problems elsewhere in their lives, often on the home front. Many of them have a problem with marijuana, he says, but only because it's a distraction from their otherwise crummy lives. It's not an addiction per se, but an escape. It's a problem in the sense that it's impossible in most cases to teach a kid that's high as a kite, but it's more a symptom than problem. Society doesn't talk too much about the root of the real problems, he says, because those are much harder to cure.

What's apparent in all of this is that teens have made a separation between pot and other drugs like coke and crack and all that Lower East Side stuff. Pot is now grouped with the legal drugs like cigarettes and booze. This is indicative of the larger, society-wide trend that sees marijuana more like Sambuca than smack.

Kids these days seem to be able to separate the wheat from the chaff, so to speak, by acknowledging the importance of the drinking and driving message, but pooh-poohing the anti-pot drivel. Their experience dictates their reality, and their reality is that booze kills their friends — pot just makes them silly. Some of these kids seem to have a better grasp of the prevalence, importance and dangers of pot than most of the adults on both sides of the war. They seem to get it into perspective.

Nelson is a tough place to live if you're 15 years old and you don't like the outdoors. If you don't ski, mountain bike or golf there is precious little to do on a Saturday night. There's a youth center, but it's become increasingly geared towards skateboarders and BMX riders. It used to be more of a place to just hang out, but the city (again led by Gary Exner) heard there was drug use going on down there and shut the place down. It re-opened under much tighter supervision and was a whole lot less fun and less popular initially, though to be fair it has picked up recently.

So what do kids do? They have bush parties and house parties and drink and smoke and get high. It's been going on for generations. It might seem worse because the media talks about these things now, brings them into the public eye instead of the wink wink that went on for years. But is it really any worse?

Kids in Nelson seem just fine, thank you very much. Despite the prevalence of dope and marijuana culture, Nelson test scores, drop-out rates and scholarship numbers are excellent when compared against the rest of B.C., and particularly good when compared to other small towns. Yes, teens smoke drugs and they drink and they get in trouble. But pot isn't ruining their lives and they certainly don't think they need to be protected and coddled by the powers that be. Like always, they just want to figure it out for themselves.

187

21
Doctor Dope

Francis is a 40-ish multiple sclerosis sufferer in Nelson who has turned to marijuana to relieve his symptoms when they occur.

"I think it's really good for stress and for being able to enjoy a good night's sleep. It helps with pain and the legal drugs I'm on now have side effects and I find pot helps with the nausea they cause."

His use has already had consequences. Francis was employed at a prominent local business when he was dismissed for what management called "failure to perform duties."

"That was the official version, but I heard it through the grapevine that the reason they canned me was because I smelled like marijuana smoke sometimes."

Francis acknowledges that smoking on the job wasn't a great idea, but says that it didn't affect his ability to his duties. As a regular smoker of herb for two decades, he says he's learned to function while under the influence. He also points out that he probably would have had to take sick time if he hadn't smoked while on the job. He has since started a home-based business that enables him to set his own hours, and he jokes that the boss doesn't mind if he takes a toke now and again.

"I've tried everything under the sun for my condition and I've found something that works for me. Why should I give it up?"

Francis says he has no intention of applying for a medical exemption because of the publicity he feels it would generate. He believes that enough people in the community are aware of his condition — including some members of the local constabulary — that there is little risk of him ever facing criminal prosecution.

"It's not like I need to look too hard to find a source," he says with a smile. Francis says he doesn't use the local compassion club simply because he doesn't want to be associated with something so indiscreet. In a small town, walking into that place is enough to get stigmatized and Francis wishes to remain as anonymous as possible about his marijuana use.

190

"This is between me and my body. It's not anybody else's business — not the cops, not the government, not Holy Smoke. I don't want to be a poster child, I just want to go about my business. It really isn't a big deal."

The medicinal use of marijuana has a long and storied history, but just because cultures used bud for medicine in days gone by doesn't necessarily validate it as a legitimate health aid, today. Relatively modern medicine is littered with strange ideas and old wives' tales. The true scientific legitimacy of marijuana has been greatly debated and there is a lot misinformation on both sides. Medical marijuana advocates — like those at Holy Smoke — are often closely associated with the decriminalization movement, allowing critics of medicinal use to claim that it is simply a smokescreen for the eventual goal of non-medicinal use. Conversely, those who argue against medical marijuana — like cops — often do so because they dislike ganja under any circumstances, regardless of the potential merits in treating patients. Like many other debates surrounding cannabis, the medical argument is generally a philosophical one, as opposed to one addressing the legitimate pros and cons. True to form, it is littered with propaganda and informational manipulation that has become the defining factor in the fight both for and against drugs. With the disclaimer that this is not a medical text, here is an attempt to sift through the litany of facts and fiction out there and break it down for the medical marijuana neophyte.

First of all, pot is bad for you. Like tobacco it has tar, carbon and other nasty substances that affect health on a long-term basis. The good news is that most studies indicate an individual would have to smoke a boatload of pot over an extended period of time to feel the negative effects. Unlike most commercially sold cigarettes, marijuana is rarely smoked with a filter, resulting in more damaging substances being transmitted to the lungs. Conversely, however, most good marijuana has fewer additional chemicals in it than cigarettes, some of which have an extraordinary number of unhealthy additives. In the Kootenays, with its health consciousness, it is actually possible to find organically grown bud. Hydroponic marijuana, however, often contains additives derived from the fertilizers and pesticides used to enhance and speed up growth.

Another factor to keep in mind when comparing the ill effects of marijuana and cigarettes is that while the average tobacco smoker might smoke as little as five or as many as 50 cigarettes in a day, even a heavy pot user would only smoke maybe three joints a day. The typical recreational user would smoke much less than that. There also seems to be some merit to the theory that smoking dope through a bong, thereby filtering it through water, helps eliminate some of the carcinogens. New age vaporizers are even better, but the technology is in its infancy and still pricey.

There is the claim that marijuana causes brain damage, particularly over a long period of time. The oft-quoted study that forwards this conclusion was done by Dr. Robert Heath, in the late 1970s. This study was reviewed by a distinguished panel of scientists sponsored by the Institute of Medicine and the National Academy of Sciences. Their results were published under the title, "Marijuana and Health" in 1982. Heath's study consisted of bombarding monkeys with high concentrations of marijuana smoke over a short period of time and came under fire for, among other things, its limited sample size. Actual studies of human populations of marijuana users have shown no evidence of brain damage. For example, two studies from 1977 published in the *Journal of the American Medical Association* (JAMA) showed no evidence of brain damage in heavy users of marijuana. That same year, the American Medical Association (AMA) officially came out in favor of decriminalizing marijuana.

Other claims against marijuana, often made by law enforcement agencies, such as it causes rapidly changing emotions, reckless or erratic behavior, distortion of time and images, altered sense of identity, hallucinations, fantasies, and paranoia, have absolutely no scientific basis. It is simply propaganda used in the war on drugs.

There are also claims that pot is a "gateway" drug, that it leads to other harder drugs like coke and heroin. There is no scientific, physiological evidence to back this up either. Surveys indicate while close to half the North American population has tried pot, less than 5 per cent has tried "hard" drugs. Neither the American or Canadian medical association categorize pot as a "narcotic", and scientific studies have shown that it is less addictive than either alcohol or commercial tobacco. On the other hand, anecdotal evidence from police and from hard drug addicts is consistent in that many users started with marijuana and alcohol and moved on to progressively more powerful substances from there. It follows a predictable line: from alcohol and cigarettes to pot, to low-level hallucinogens like mushrooms and peyote, to more substantial hallucinogens like LSD (acid). Many consistent marijuana users — including the Holy Smoke owners — have done some kind of experimentation with those types of substances. There seems to be a barrier between that level and the next, far more dangerous order of drugs which include heroin and cocaine. The new age of drugs, the so-called "lifestyle" drugs such as crystal meth and ecstasy, are in a league all their own, and few serious marijuana users, particularly in the Kootenays, seem to bother with them.

One of the most common comparisons by legalization advocates is between marijuana and alcohol. At the root, pot is less lethal than booze. The killer dose of alcohol, as compared to the dosage needed to get intoxicated, is somewhere in the neighborhood of between six and ten to one. That means if an individual needed to drink 12 ounces of rye to get intoxicated, that same individual might be dead if they drank a sixty pounder all by themselves — and they would definitely be dead if they drank two. The ratio for pot is closer to 40,000 to one, meaning the average stoner would need to smoke 40,000 joints to kill themselves. Good luck.

193

Unlike alcohol, tere is no scientific or even anecdotal evidence that pot makes people violent. In fact studies and the courts have held that marijuana has the opposite effect. Think about the stereotypes in this case: pot smokers are seen as peace loving, couch bound, popcorn munching, easygoing folks. Now compare that to your average frat house. The general conception is that those that abuse alcohol are far more likely to be violent than your average pot smokers. Police, however, will point to studies showing that close to 25 per cent of all inmates serving federal time in Canada had marijuana in their system when they committed their crimes. What they don't offer is what percentage of those also had alcohol in their bloodstreams at the time.

What about the idea that pot is "mentally addictive" or that it leads to a certain lackadaisical lifestyle — often referred to as amotivational syndrome? Though there is plenty of anecdotal evidence to give this claim credence, it is also easily debunked. This is a bit of a chicken or the egg argument: are stoners lazy because they're stoned all the time, or are they stoned all the time because they are lazy? There is no scientific evidence to prove that being a pot head will make you a skid as well. If you are naturally lacking in motivation, however, pot certainly won't help.

Scientifically substantiated claims for the benefits of marijuana are many. The two most common are as an anti-nauseant and as an appetite inducer. It is used by many people undergoing chemotherapy and radiotherapy for cancers or suffering from AIDS. The majority (83% at last survey) of Canadian oncologists would prescribe marijuana to some of their patients were it legal. Health Canada has now approved this use. A large minority (43% at last survey) of Canadian oncologists have recommended pot to some of their patients despite its illegality. As a appetite inducer, pot is legendary, even among recreational users, for bringing on the munchies. For people with eating disorders, or again suffering from the side-effects of cancer treatment or AIDS, marijuana can be helpful in making them want to eat. Health Canada has also approved this use.

Marijuana is also used as a pain-killer for those suffering from migraines and back pain and by MS patients as an antispastic. Though the benefits for those uses are not scientifically clear, the anecdotal evidence is substantial.

There is a pharmaceutical version of dope, called Marinol, that is prescribed primarily for cancer patients. It is the good part of marijuana, THC, and is often taken orally as a pill. While it has proved effective in many cases, it is seen by some as inferior to marijuana because of the time it takes to be effective and the fact that there are other medicinal elements contained with marijuana that Marinol doesn't include. THC is only one of over 460 substances in dope and only one of the 21 cannibinols.

Medicinal marijuana has enjoyed a resurgence of late. In the spring of 1999 the Canadian minister of health announced the federal government would begin conducting clinical trials on the value of medicinal marijuana. Several cases of possession of marijuana for medicinal use have been tossed out by the courts. The health minister has granted several exemptions under the Controlled Drugs and Substances Act, allowing for people to use medical marijuana without being charged.

While this is seen as a victory by many who favor medicinal marijuana, it has put law enforcement and even those who receive an exemption in a difficult position — for while it is legal for people with an exemption to possess marijuana, they still can't cultivate it and there is no legitimate source to purchase it from. A well-publicized case was the woman from Ontario who had her marijuana, which she had purchased from a compassion club in B.C., confiscated by police when it arrived.

195

Another Ontario man with an exemption has petitioned the government to provide him with a safe source of high-quality, chemical-free marijuana because the product available to him through conventional sources is inadequate. The government is reportedly pondering the request.

"I heard they are looking to the States for a source of high-quality, organic marijuana," says one Kootenay grower. "What a joke. I have some in my basement."

These developments have, predictably, sparked debate on the wisdom of letting people smoke pot and added fuel to the decriminalization fire. In Nelson, the Holy Smokers have used this window to further their cause by establishing the Kootenay Compassion Club, one of several popping up all over the country. The spiritual, greed-free approach of many of the area's growers, whose holistic approach to growing emphasizes quality, is a good match.

The expertise of the dope growers in the community is another asset. Their ability to breed complex strains of marijuana for a specific purpose — in most cases to increase the speed of growth and the yield of bud — can also be applied to growing marijuana for specific medical ailments.

"We've bred different strains in this area that are better for certain ailments," says one grower. "It's certainly not hard."

For the Holy Smoke crew, access to medicinal marijuana is another element in their fight towards decriminalization. Preventing the sick from recieving a substance that could alleviate their suffering is another example of what they see as arcane laws that hurt instead of help the average citizen.

"The highest thing that a society can be based on is compassion because that means that society cares for people and cares for the sick. So for the government to deny medicinal cannabis is uncompassionate ... so it would seem we are heading in the right direction if compassion is the highest ideal," Cantwell says.

In the summer of 2000, the Nelson Cannabis Compassion Club separated itself from the depths of the Holy Smoke Culture Shop location and branched out on its own. It now has its own non-profit status and an office a couple of blocks away.

Coordinator Phil McMillan sells pot to patients over the counter, an act which is still technically illegal. But instead of being concerned about arrest, he wants to reach out to Nelson City Police.

"I'm wanting to connect with the police — I want a liaison officer to work with me on this, so that if they pull over someone with marijuana and see identification issued by me, they won't arrest anybody, and they'll return any pot they seize, because it would be cruel not to," said McMillan says.

McMillan, who was a social worker in Vancouver for eight years before moving to Nelson, sells pot for $20/30 per eighth of an ounce to those who can provide a doctor's note saying they suffer from a medical condition.

Some of his 40 or so clients suffer from AIDS and various forms of cancer, says McMillan, who buys the organic bud from family-run grow operations.

"I've never had to buy from any criminal organizations. There's just too many mom-and-pop organizations around town for that to be a problem," said McMillan.

McMillan hopes to eventually grow his own marijuana legally, and to see laws that permit medicinal use of marijuana formally recognized.

Which is already happening.

A monumental court decision destined to change the fate of marijuana in Canada came trundling down the pipe on July 31, 2000 when the Ontario Court of Appeal struck down the law prohibiting possession.

This does not mean the masses are now free to carry bud on their person without fear, however. The court gave Ottawa a year to fix the law, keeping the existing law in place until then.

The case involved 44-year-old Terry Parker, who says marijuana has virtually eliminated the 15 to 80 weekly seizures he suffered for about 40 years as a symptom of his epilepsy.

The ruling, written by judges Marvin Catzman, Louise Charron and Marc Rosenberg, was part of a decision which upheld a lower court judge's decision that has allowed Parker to legally smoke pot for the past three years.

It is an important decision for several reasons. It acknowledges that marijuana has legitimate medicinal value and that the law is based on faulty misconceptions. It states that the exemption offered by the federal government are doled out in an unfair manner. Most important, it says that Parker's Charter Rights are violated by the Controlled Drugs and Substances Act.

"Forcing Parker to choose between his health and imprisonment violates his right to liberty and security of person," Justice Rosenberg wrote in the court's decision.

Predictably, medicinal pot advocates were happy with the decision.

"The decision will open doors across the country for sick Canadians who need pot to help alleviate symptoms such as nausea and vomiting," said Parker's lawyer, Aaron Harnett.

Multiple sclerosis sufferer Alison Myrden smokes a joint every two hours. She says that eight years ago she had no use of her lower body and was confined to a wheelchair, suffering from nerve pain, bladder incontinence and muscle spasms and popping 30 pills a day, including 600 mg of morphine. Now she just smokes pot.

"I'm absolutely overjoyed. It's a huge victory for us," said Myrden.

While support from users is certainly not a shocker, the ruling also received support from mainstream media and right-wing think tanks the Fraser Institute. In the opinion piece, "A victory for sensible drug policy," the Institute's Patrick Basham lays it out:

> The court's judgement reflected what's been conclusively and repeatedly demonstrated: marijuana serves as a tremendously helpful appetite stimulant or pain reliever to patients afflicted with epilepsy, AIDS, cancer, glaucoma,

or multiple sclerosis. Prior to yesterday's ruling, only 50 Canadians were legally entitled to smoke marijuana. Now, an estimated 150,000 people in Ontario alone could benefit from the medical use of marijuana.

Opposition stems from a combination of ignorance and well-intentioned, if misplaced, moralism which argues that medical marijuana promotes drug experimentation and abuse. Suffice it to say, both the historical and scientific evidence demonstrate otherwise.

The standard government line remains that there's no official evidence marijuana helps ease patients' symptoms. After all, as US deputy drug czar Dr. Don Vereen noted, "Smoked marijuana has not been tested (by the government)." Fortunately, judicial wisdom and medical expertise is overcoming such political intransigence north and south of the border.

Nothing like smarty-pants, two-dollar word, arch-conservatives jumping on the weed wagon.

It is important to note, however, that the court does not advocate the use of recreational marijuana. In another ruling released the same day, the court upheld a lower court decision that prevents Chris Clay, a London, Ontario, man from possessing pot for recreational purposes. Clay had been seeking to legalize recreational marijuana, claiming that pot has no harmful side effects and that criminalization of the drug poses a greater danger to the public.

But there's little question the heat is on the feds. If Ottawa fails to change the law — as they did when the Supreme Court of Canada struck down a criminal ban on abortion in 1986 — marijuana possession will be legal in Ontario by mid-2001, and the rest of the country soon after.

For Dustin Cantwell, the Compassion Club has taken on a personal meaning. At the end of 1999, his mother was diag-

199

nosed with a brain tumor and underwent serious chemotherapy. Cantwell returned to Ontario to tend to her and said that
for the first time in her life, his mom used marijuana, to com-
bat the nausea.

"Here's a woman that never approved of drug use, not ever.
But when things got bad for her and she couldn't eat, I said,
'Mom this will help.' She was desperate and she tried it and it
has made her more comfortable," he says.

Those themes — desperation and comfort — recur commonly in those who are seeking relief through marijuana.

Conclusion and Epilogue

*T*here are several lessons to be drawn from the Nelson-area marijuana trade, both in the specifics and as it applies to North America as a whole. While Nelson is certainly unique in its bud trade and culture, it is still, at its root, a microcosm of the larger picture.

First, Holy Smoke. The truth of whether the Nelson City Police planted evidence in order to frame the owners and put the shop out of business will never be known. Miller, to this day, denies it and has lasting emotional scars from the experience.

"The judge basically called me a liar. It was very painful. It's still painful right now. I don't know how he could come to that conclusion. Totally wrong. I'm still emotional about it. I was angry, I was hurt. I was embarrassed: embarrassed for me, for my family, for my department, for my community. I thought I let people down and I didn't know what I did. I'm not above making mistakes but I definitely didn't here. I definitely didn't stage the evidence. Totally wrong. A big mistake on the judge's part.

"I'm a very proud man, I love my job, I love this community. I would never do anything to jeopardize those things and my family. I'm not the most educated guy around, but I think people could always say you could count on me, that you could trust me. Up until that decision anyway. It was awkward for me to walk around town for a while. I'm over that now, but it's still painful.

"Am I going to jeopardize my career, this investigation, this community, based on, what? A baggie of dope? Not likely."

Everyone — including criminals who know Miller — were shocked by the ruling. Miller had had an unimpeachable record until this case. He seems to have been undone by one simple omission: his failure to take pictures of the central piece of evidence that the search warrant was based on. Miller rightly points out that the photos are not a requirement of law — that his word should have been enough.

202

But Justice Mark Takahashi, and the other judges in the Kootenays, seem to be developing a cynicism towards the behavior of police, based in no small part on the fact that officers have been stretching the bounds of the law to get warrants and convictions. There seems to be little doubt that some police officers, frustrated by the number and boldness of grow ops are willing to skirt the corners of the law — and judges are calling them on it.

On the other hand, the police feel increasingly isolated in their fight against marijuana. While cultivation, trafficking and possession are still crimes, the police feel they are being given insufficient resources to make a dent in the problem. They feel embarrassed by the situation. To make matters worse, when they do haul growers and traffickers before the courts they watch them get off with a minimum penalty. The cops are in no-man's land.

But that frustration does not justify violations of the Charter of Rights and Freedoms. Those laws, it should be pointed out, do not exist to protect dope growers but to protect the average law-abiding citizen from unreasonable harassment and search. Judge Takahashi wasn't defending Holy Smoke or their lifestyle choice, he was defending the basic tenets of the legal system that shield us all.

And it should be pointed out that whether or not the cops planted evidence against Holy Smoke, there is little question that there was a law enforcement and political conspiracy to try and run them out of town. From Scalia's memo to Mayor Gary Exner's selective manipulation of the business license fee structure, the powers that be were out to get Holy Smoke. That effort in itself is hugely problematic. The Machiavellian efforts by governments and guys with guns to target specific people because of their decision to exercise free speech or choose a lifestyle that does not meet the standards of those in power has dire implications.

203

On the flip side, however, there is no question that the owners of the Holy Smoke Culture Shop were — and are — breaking the law. The cops could go in there tomorrow and find people smoking dope, and dope on the premises. While they talked big at the time of the bust about changing the marijuana laws in Canada, when push came to shove the owners of Holy Smoke beat this rap on a technicality and nothing more glamorous than that.

The presence of young people in the store continues to be a concern for the police, the politicians and for the general public that would otherwise be willing to let Holy Smoke continue on its ganja way. While Holy Smokers continue to deny — and have always denied — that they sell drugs or paraphernalia to minors, the rumors persist that such sales do indeed take place. Without question, minors have been allowed to enter the store and nose around, perhaps even smoking their own herb in the daily five o'clock "prayer session." In this regard, Const. Bill Clay is right: Holy Smoke would put a lot of people at ease and make their own lives much easier by barring entry to anyone under the age of 19.

Not that it would have a substantial impact on the prevalence or availability of marijuana in the lives of the young people of Nelson. The good news is that they seem to be better equipped to handle it than ever before.

Which should put Ernie Miller at ease. Shortly after the Holy Smoke case concluded, Constable Ernie became Sergeant Ernie, debunking any theories that Miller's career would be damaged by Takahashi's harsh words. He continues to enjoy the support of his fellow officers, the community and even the marijuana community, who see him as a fair-minded guy just doing his job.

Miller's promotion coincided with the one received by Frank Scalia, who moved from Sergeant to Inspector. Scalia, who continues to be the harshest and most outspoken critic of marijuana and the Holy Smoke Culture Shop, is now second in command and considered the frontrunner to succeed Andrew Oak as chief of the Nelson City Police.

Ken Hammond, convicted of the murder of Shaun Britton and the best example of the fact there is some marijuana-related violence in the Kootenays, lost his appeal and is now facing the prospect of serving his full sentence — life behind bars.

But Hammond's case continues to be an anomaly in an otherwise peaceful marijuana-growing industry. Despite the allegation by law enforcement that marijuana is a business controlled or influenced by organized crime, Asian gangs or biker groups, there is absolutely no evidence that those factors are at play in the Kootenays. It is a trade dominated by no specific group, but those most prevalent — the mom and pop basement grower and the young hippie for which marijuana is a spiritual experience for example — are beyond benign. Nelson is a quiet town where people keep their doors unlocked during the day. Considering the volume of illegal enterprise going on, that is truly remarkable.

The Holy Smoke Culture Shop continues to trundle on — still looking to turn a profit. Alan Middlemiss left the business in early 2000, moving to Manitoba in order to be closer to his ex-wife and his two children. Middlemiss's involvement with the shop and his lifestyle choices were an issue in his acrimonious divorce from a woman who has found the Lord and now frowns on marijuana.

"I was deemed a marijuana addict by my ex-partner. I might be mentally dependent at very worst, but physically addicted — no way," he says. They settled and Middlemiss has joint custody.

He now works on an organic farm and promotes marijuana decriminalization in a far more subtle way — rural Manitoba doesn't have the same tolerance as Nelson. He misses the bud life.

205

"It was completely a life choice to be with my kids. But those guys [Cantwell and DeFelice] are my partners, my friends, my brothers. I would love to still be there."

Dustin "Sunflower" Cantwell and Paul DeFelice still work at the store, though DeFelice continues to draft on the side.

As for another bust, that seems unlikely. After the fiasco that was the first trial, neither the city nor the NCP seems particularly interested in stirring up the Holy Smoke hornet's nest. In a tolerant town, the ends simply don't justify the means. Ernie Miller, however, says he would like one more kick at the can.

"If they're doing things illegally, if they're selling drugs, yeah I want to shut them down. But I haven't heard anything since. Doesn't mean they're not. I want to get them just like anybody else that is involved with marijuana — that's the law. Not just because of who they are, but because of what they're doing."